#WHATIS

#WHATIS
A NEAR-DEATH
EXPERIENCE?

DR PENNY SARTORI

This edition published in the UK and USA 2016 by
Watkins, an imprint of Watkins Media Limited
19 Cecil Court
London WC2N 4EZ

enquiries@watkinspublishing.co.uk

Design and typography copyright © Watkins Media Limited 2016

Text copyright © Penny Sartori 2016

10 9 8 7 6 5 4 3 2 1

Typeset by Manisha Patel

Printed and bound in Germany by GGP Media GmbH

A CIP record for this book is available from the British Library

ISBN: 978-1-78028-898-7

www.watkinspublishing.com

CONTENTS

Why read this book?

My aim in writing this book is to provide an accessible guide to Near-Death Experiences (NDEs) for anyone who would like to learn more about them. Most people have heard of NDEs but the common features of these events and their meaning in the context of our lives are often shrouded in mystery. I passionately believe that NDEs have something to teach all of us, even if we have never ourselves had a near-death experience or anything like it.

20 reasons to start reading!

This book will help you to ...

1 Learn the major features and defining characteristics of NDEs as compared with other spiritual experiences.

2 Learn the difference between NDEs and out-of-body experiences.

3 Learn from the stories of those who have experienced an NDE.

4 Learn to identify an NDE if someone you meet describes one for you.

5 Discover how to validate the NDE experience for someone who's had one.

6 Better understand the dying process, and the importance of dying with dignity.

7 Release your fear of death, and help others release theirs.

8 Improve your powers of empathy and understanding.

9 Challenge yourself to explore your own mortality.

10 Learn the importance of living mindfully – understanding how every moment matters.

11 See how your own actions impact upon those around you.

12 Consider the interconnectivity of all living things – humans, animals and the Earth.

13 Explore the nature of consciousness, and what it means to be conscious or unconscious.

14 Feel inspired to show love and compassion in all your undertakings and relationships.

15 Consider how learning about NDEs can help improve our healthcare provision.

16 Reflect on different cultures and belief systems – exploring both their similarities and differences – and how that manifests in experience of NDEs.

17 Consider your wishes for your own life and death, and how you wish to be treated as you die.

18 Become more open to talking about death frankly with those around you.

19 Enjoy the experience of expanding your understanding of spirituality in general.

20 Be inspired to delve further into this fascinating subject.

From this list you can see that I want to inspire you to consider NDEs as a learning tool for your own life. That applies as much to those who've never had an NDE as it does to those who have. I want to motivate you not only to further your knowledge of NDEs, but also to consider other, related aspects of spirituality. A spark of interest in NDEs can lead to an exploration of your own mortality and consciousness, as well as to an investigation of your own spiritual beliefs and how you formed them. Spirituality gives life meaning – it inspires us to live happy and fulfilled lives. It is not the same as religion, which is a doctrine – a set of given principles to adopt and interpret in light of your own circumstances. Spirituality invites you to seek your own life truths and to apply them to your life in order that they fulfil you.

Key features of this book

In the Introduction I explain how I became interested in NDEs as a nurse and the story of my subsequent research and work with NDErs around the world. Chapter 1 sets out the characteristics of NDEs, while Chapter 2 explores whether NDEs are pleasant or distressing experiences. Chapter 3 looks at the circumstances that can lead to NDEs, and who has them, while Chapter 4 reveals how NDEs change lives. Chapter 5 delves into the science of NDEs, highlighting the latest medical research into the phenomenon. The final chapters of the book look at what we can learn from NDEs, how we can be more sympathetic toward those who've had them, and what a greater understanding of these experiences could mean for humankind as a whole.

This book is designed to make NDEs as accessible as possible, with the help of the following features:

- A Q&A approach that chapter by chapter explores the questions that are often asked about NDEs.
- 'Case Study' boxes that share real-life experiences of NDEs.
- 'Focus On' boxes that suggest practical ways of putting the lessons learned from NDErs into practice in everyday life.
- At the end of the book, a 'What Next' section, including a further reading list, suggests how to continue your investigations – there is so much more to say about NDEs and there are so many more fascinating things to learn.

KEY ABBREVIATIONS

The following abbreviations are used throughout the book for key terms:

NDE – near-death experience
NDEr – near-death experiencer
OBE – out-of-body experience
DBV – deathbed vision
STE – spiritually transformative experience

INTRODUCTION

Why this subject?

For many, death is a taboo subject. We might think that death is for other people – perhaps the ill or the elderly – and not our concern. Until, that is, something drastic happens: perhaps our own diagnosis of terminal illness, a near-miss accident, or the death of someone we love. Given that death is the only certainty in life, it is strange that we rarely spend time thinking about it. Paradoxically, though, when we do contemplate what it means to die and we think about the process of dying, we open ourselves to discovering the essentials of living a fulfilled, connected life.

After a brush with death, many people report experiences they find hard to put into words. This tongue-tie is often because what happened felt like no experience they'd ever had before. How can any of us describe something for which we have no tangible frame of reference? And if we can't ourselves understand that experience, or expect that anyone else has been through it, how can we share it? The term for an experience that occurs in the moments between life and death is a 'near-death experience', or an NDE. Historically, many of those who've had one have been reluctant to talk about it. That's something I want to change.

Advances in healthcare mean that, year on year, far more people are surviving cardiac arrest and critical illness than ever before. It is therefore highly likely that the numbers of people encountering NDEs will also increase. The information about NDEs offered in the following pages will, I hope, help all of us understand such experiences better, with both the experiencers (the NDErs) and those of us who hear NDE accounts benefiting from improved understanding. Learning from others who have been affected by NDEs can lead to great insights into the impermanence of life. This knowledge is incredibly empowering, helping us to enjoy our lives while we have them, and soothing away our fears relating to death.

Why me?

I began a 21-year nursing career in 1989. At the start I worked throughout the hospital, in various departments, but eventually I found my vocation in intensive care, where I nursed for 17 years. Here, I was confronted with death on such a frequent basis I had no choice but to face up to the single certainty that death comes to everyone. It does not care for age (it is not only for the elderly), and sometimes it takes us entirely by surprise (it is not only for the ill). During my career I nursed thousands of patients through their deaths; and I've nursed loved ones at the end of their lives, too.

Early on in my career, as I cared for a dying patient, an upsetting encounter threw me into a deep depression that forced me to question life and death. Soon after I read a book about NDEs. I was filled with preconceived ideas and scepticism, but the book opened a sense of fascination within me and drew me to find out more. As a result I undertook the UK's first long-term prospective study of NDEs at the intensive therapy unit (ITU) where I worked. I spent five years interviewing patients who survived their admission to the ITU, asking them if they had any memories of the time during which they were unconscious. Then, after eight years of intense doctoral study, in 2005 I was awarded a PhD. It is more than 20 years since my fascination with NDEs began, and I have lectured at conferences all over the world and amassed a database of hundreds of accounts of NDEs. I believe I have a duty to share my knowledge in order to help other people understand what NDEs are and why they are so important.

Why now?

This book feels timely to me as we are increasingly open-minded about the links between mind, body and spirit. Recent years have seen greater acceptance of spirituality in general and especially in relation to patient care in hospitals. We are lucky to be able to benefit from powerful technology and deep scientific understanding of life and death, but we also now realize how important the spiritual aspects of life are to our overall well-being.

When I began my research more than 20 years ago, it was very difficult to find someone who was willing to talk to me about their NDE. Many people were wary of me (would I question their mental health?), others struggled to put their experience into words, and some simply did not want to share this deeply personal aspect of themselves. Gradually, as people got to hear about my work, more and more of them made contact with me. Nonetheless, when my book *The Wisdom of NDEs* was published in 2014, I was not prepared for the huge response it would receive.

A few weeks prior to the book's launch, my publisher called me to say that a national newspaper was going to feature my text in two articles. My initial reaction was one of alarm: how would the general public respond to my research? By the end of the day in which the first article was published, social media saw to it that my book was known all over the world. The majority of the comments I received were very positive. In itself, this made me realize that attitudes toward NDEs (and spiritual experiences in general) had changed a lot since my research began. Furthermore, the article encouraged many people to talk about their own experiences. Instead of the two articles originally planned five were published, one featuring the accounts of NDErs who were willing to share their stories publicly, alongside their photographs. It was a breakthrough.

During the first few weeks following my book's publication, I received around 200 emails a day from NDErs all over the world. More than a year later, I still receive hundreds of emails a week. But it's not just that people who've experienced an NDE are more comfortable than ever before talking about their experiences – there's also a healthy curiosity about NDE among those who've never had the experience themselves. Slowly, we're learning that perhaps science does not have all the answers. In fact, there is much we can learn from NDEs that we can apply to our everyday lives, regardless of whether or not we have first-hand knowledge of this particular spiritual phenomenon.

Now is an exciting time to be exploring further what it means to be human in life, death, and consciousness. I hope that the information in the following pages helps you on this journey.

CHAPTER 1

What are the features of NDEs, and are NDEs the same as OBEs?

NDEs transcend all other human experience; they are more than physical occurrences, being more numinous or mystical in nature. Many people imagine that NDEs must be dreamlike, but this is not the case. A dream is transitory and often vague, whereas NDEs result in *heightened* states of awareness: the senses become more acute – colours may appear more vibrant, smells may be more vivid, and sounds may become audible over otherwise impossible distances. Often the NDEr may become aware of events that are occurring in a different location. It can be an extraordinary, overwhelming experience that leaves the NDEr facing important life changes.

Do NDEs have any shared features?

NDEs usually occur spontaneously and unexpectedly, when someone is genuinely near death or during a life-threatening situation (see case study, pages 22–3), so it may take a while for the person to realize what is going on. No two NDEs that I have ever heard of are the same, although many share certain characteristics and go on to result in significant life changes (which we'll talk about later in the chapter).

The most common characteristics or themes were first identified by Dr Raymond Moody in 1975 in his book *Life After Life* (see the list, opposite). Not every NDE comprises all of these components – some may have just one or two.

Characteristics or themes may come and go, and don't necessarily occur in any order. Some may be intricate and in-depth, others may be simple.

This list summarizes Moody's findings about the most commonly shared features of NDEs:

• Hearing the news of being close to death (or of being dead)
• Hearing 'white' noise
• Having an out-of-body experience (OBE)
• Experiencing feelings of peace and tranquillity
• Travelling through a dark tunnel
• Seeing a bright light
• Entering another realm
• Meeting those who have already died
• Meeting a 'Being of Light'
• Communicating without words
• Experiencing a 'life review'
• Feeling a sense of unity or interconnectivity
• Experiencing distortion of time
• Coming to a barrier or point of no return
• Being sent back to life

All the points on this list are explored in more detail on pages 24–9.

CASESTUDY NDE IN A LIFE-THREATENING SITUATION

'My NDE occurred during the 2004 tsunami. There was
no great visual journey, there were no voices and so on. It
was simply a sensation, a feeling ... After the initial terror, and
a sense of "knowing" that this is how I was going to die, the
water momentarily seemed to form a cooling, comforting
cushion around me before starting to throw me about in
the bamboo hut, like a rag doll in a washing machine.
Everything went into slow motion and a sense of calm swept
over me. Everything was fine. Everything was okay. All was
just as it was meant to be.

'In those moments I had an overwhelming sensation that
there was nothing to fear. Nothing to worry about. I was
lucky. I had led a good life. I had loved and felt loved. And
all the worrying I had done about things both small and big
in my life was washed way. I felt at peace and, weirdly, I felt
still, despite being tumbled wildly around in the water, not
knowing which way was the "top".

'It's the calmest and clearest I've ever felt. So much so that
I find it hard to describe. The closest I can manage is to
say that it felt like I was surrounded by and filled with pure
love and contentment. A deep sense that everything was

interconnected and perfect. And that all I had to do was accept whatever happened. It would all be all right.

'I couldn't see the turmoil or destruction going on around me. All I could sense was light. And when I finally found the "top" I was incredulous that there was just enough space in the hut for me to lift my mouth out of the water and take the deepest and most grateful breath I've ever taken before deciding which way I should swim to try to get out.

'I saw another wall of water sweeping toward me and then I must have blacked out. The next thing I knew I had surfaced some distance from the hut. A new part of the ordeal – the much more drawn-out part of it – was about to start: swimming but not getting anywhere, being lifted up into a tree by a Thai man, trying to get to shore, searching for my partner, realizing just how injured he was when I did find him, trying to get to high land and a place of safety and shelter, tending to my partner's serious wounds, trying to get to a hospital on the mainland and having to fight for medical treatment among the chaos when we finally got there ... The trauma and terror had only just begun. But in the process, during those few minutes, or however long it was in the water, I'd had an experience that would change how I view life, and to a large extent death, for ever.'

Hearing the news of being close to death

Some NDErs report having heard a bystander saying that they have had a cardiac arrest (for example), or that they are already dead. It may take the NDErs a few minutes to realize the bystander is talking about them.

Hearing 'white' noise

Although noise may not feature at all in some NDEs, many NDErs describe their experience as beginning with a crackling or hissing noise, or sometimes a ringing or buzzing.

Having an out-of-body experience (OBE)

Sometimes NDErs find themselves floating around the room, near to the ceiling, and sometimes the ceiling appears to have disappeared. In many cases the person doesn't even realize that the body they are looking down on from above is their own body. It may come as a shock when eventually the realization dawns that they are out of their own body.

Experiencing feelings of peace and tranquillity

This is one of the most common features of NDEs. Despite the often traumatic circumstances leading up to the experience, most people remark how wonderful an NDE feels. These feelings are often associated with great joy and the disappearance of any pain.

Travelling through a dark tunnel

Some NDEs feature a transition from darkness into light, often described as travelling through a dark tunnel. In some non-Western cultures the dark tunnel is replaced with a path.

Seeing a bright light

Light in NDEs often has a certain quality – warm and comfortable, or 'magnetic', drawing the NDEr toward it. NDErs may report that bright light does not hurt the eyes. Light may appear as a tiny pinprick and grow into a large expanse.

Entering another realm

Many NDErs feel as if they have moved into another world. For example, NDErs have described to me scenes of a beautiful flower garden, or a stream with a bridge across it.

Meeting those who have already died

Deceased relatives, friends or acquaintances feature frequently in NDE accounts. Dead pets also sometimes feature, especially in the NDEs of children. The NDEr may meet someone whom they didn't know had died – and only learns of the death after they themselves have been revived.

Meeting a 'Being of Light'

The 'Being of Light' that appears in some NDEs has been variously described as a religious figure, an angel or just a presence. The form of any religious figure is usually informed by the NDEr's cultural heritage. For example, Christians usually describe images of Jesus, but Hindus are more likely to describe Yama, the god of death, or the *yamdoots*, his messengers. The NDEr usually reports a great sense of love and comfort emanating from this presence.

Communicating without words

Any communication that occurs during NDEs (perhaps with someone who has already died, or with a 'Being of Light') is often described as a non-verbal, direct transference of thought. Many people report that they did not once see the mouth of the deceased or Being move, yet were instantly able to understand what they were being told.

Experiencing a 'life review'

Perhaps the most complex component of many NDEs, the life review is particularly fascinating because it can be so deep and detailed (see case study, page 28). Some report that the review occurs from a third-person perspective, enabling the NDEr to feel first-hand the impact of their own actions (good and bad) on other people. They may relive experiences that otherwise they'd forgotten about, or that at the time seemed irrelevant. NDErs who've had a life review suggest that it can be a particularly traumatic aspect of the NDE. Many say they are accompanied by a presence or

'Being of Light' that acts as a source of comfort during the process. The life review seems to be one of the main triggers of real-life change following recovery from an NDE.

Feeling a sense of unity or interconnectivity

Many NDErs report a prevailing sense that we are all interconnected. The feelings of unity with others and the universe itself can dominate the experience and often carry through into everyday life.

Experiencing distortion of time

Commonly during NDEs, time seems to have no meaning; it may slow down or speed up. A person may be unconscious for only a few seconds, yet have a very intricate experience that would take many hours to replay in full.

Coming to a barrier or point of no return

In most cases the NDEr reaches a point of no return. He or she may encounter a barrier in any form – it has been variously described as a river, a gate, a doorway and a fence. Commonly, NDErs report that within the NDE they are aware that if they cross the barrier, they will not return to life. Some people recall making a conscious decision to return to life, while others recall being told they have a decision to make. In many cases those people seem not to recall making the decision itself, but simply revive in their body.

Being sent back to life

A deceased relative or Being of Light often sends the NDEr back to life, telling him or her that it is not yet their time, or that

---

CASESTUDY NDE LIFE REVIEW

Author Angie Fenimore's NDE began with a re-experience of her own birth, followed by a review of her whole life. However, it wasn't a simple matter of life 'flashing before her eyes' – the review gave her far greater insight than she'd had at the time: 'I knew exactly how each person felt who had ever interacted with me ... I easily absorbed every moment, each one triggering an entire memory or chunk of my life.' She saw her childhood in depth, recalling the important emotions of the time and how secure she had felt then. As the review moved forward into her darker years, there was less detail. The review passed over difficult events with a sense of detachment and the woman wasn't able to stay 'within' any of those later memories. She then realized that she was accompanied by a male presence that neither judged her life nor empathized with it. (You can read more about this specific NDE on pages 38–9.)

---

he or she has work to do. On coming back to life, the NDEr may have a greater sense of purpose than before, although people seldom remember what that precise purpose is.

In summary

Overall, then, we can see that the features of an NDE vary from person to person, making each experience unique. Culture, upbringing and individual circumstances may all play a part in how NDEs manifest, as well as many intangible and unidentifiable triggers of the unconscious.

Are NDEs the same as OBEs?

Other experiences, mainly out-of-body experiences (OBEs), may be confused with NDEs. As mentioned on page 24, the features of OBEs can overlap with those of NDEs. However, while OBEs can occur during NDEs, they can also occur when there is no threat of death and are therefore not in themselves NDEs. Also, OBEs can be induced, whereas NDEs never happen at will. Four case studies now look at possible OBE scenarios:

- OBE in combination with other features of NDEs
- OBE as a single feature of NDEs
- OBE with no threat of death
- Induced OBE

CASESTUDY OBE IN COMBINATION WITH OTHER FEATURES OF NDEs

In November 1984 one NDEr nearly died from malaria while living in Togo, West Africa: 'That night I had no fight left, no energy to live, no ability to move – I just wanted the pain in my head to go away, the aching and arching of my body to cease and the world to stop spinning. Too long had I been slowly dying. I turned to the wall, curled up into a comforting foetal position and thought of my family so far away.

'The next thing I knew, I was above the bathroom door opposite my single, sweat-soaked bed, looking down on my lifeless body – a shell of myself. Empty of life, a curled-up motionless adult baby. Calm, pain-free, surreal, almost happy – just not me. Soulless and still, quiet, serene and tranquil. Behind me, a bright light – so bright and inviting. There was no wall anymore that divided bathroom from bedroom – it was just a hole of light, a warming tunnel of serenity enveloping the area behind me as if I were sitting in the entrance of peace and eternal calm. But more vivid, more intimate and more touching was the hazy, familiar, smiling, moustached silhouette of my father, who had died when I was 12.

'His smell, the scent that had so often enveloped me in life, now enveloped me in my death ... I knew I had a choice ... to go to my father's arms, silhouetted and open, to where he now existed, or to return to the world of the living. My father in soul and mind was in touch with my soul and mind. It wasn't in words like we speak in our living world that he gave me the choice ... it was through the entwinement of our souls and thoughts ...

'His name for me – "dolly bird" – came to my mind. He "souled" (communicated with his soul, as opposed to told) me that he was always standing by me and I would join him at some point, but not necessarily now. The choice was mine and only I could make it. This soul conversation felt like hours, but it was ten minutes at most.

'During the time I was with my father, in real life my sister and my mother woke up and met on the landing at our farm (in England) overwhelmed with anxiety as a result of their dreams. Immediately, they called Pattie to ask if I were alive or dead. Pattie ran to my room and shook my lifeless body – at this point I was dead and a long way from my body, but I had made my choice to return ... I took a breath ... I had almost chosen to abandon my life.'

CASESTUDY OBE AS A SINGLE FEATURE OF NDE

One NDEr described an NDE with an OBE during childbirth:
'I am a nurse myself, now a midwife based in Swansea. My
experience of giving birth was a traumatic time that ended
up with me being in the High Dependency Unit (HDU) in
the labour ward ... I didn't arrest, but I did have an out-of-
body experience ... It was so real. I know it sounds like a
cliché, but I was in the corner of the room, up on the ceiling

CASESTUDY OBE WITH NO THREAT OF DEATH

This OBEr was 18 at the time of his experience and working
as a hospital technician: 'It was a Sunday afternoon and
I had attended church that morning ... Out of nowhere I
suddenly felt a huge compulsion to get on my knees and
pray. As I put my elbows on the settee, I felt myself fly out of
my body at great speed. I travelled high in the sky over the
Atlantic ocean until, about mid-ocean, I saw a large luxury
passenger boat (like the *QE2*) heading toward the USA. Like
Superman, I aimed for it at high speed. I went right through
several layers of cabins and stopped just below the ceiling
of a cabin where a couple was having an argument.

looking down at my colleagues working on me. I could see myself as well as hear what they were saying about me, yet what I was hearing was as though I was standing behind them and not lying in the bed in front of them. I heard the whispered conversation of the doctors who stood by the door to HDU, too far away for me to hear it from my bed.

This experience never frightened me, and after 11 years it is as clear today as it was then.'

No thinking on my part was involved. It just happened. Suspended there, I continued gently praying for them. All the time I was aware that my physical body was kneeling in Bristol and that a very fine silver-coloured line linked that body with my soul thousands of miles away. Fairly quickly the couple calmed down. Then I started to be slightly uneasy about being in two places at once and I thought I'd rather be back in Bristol. I began to hurtle back down the silver line. When very close to my body, I had a brief blackout moment. Then I was back in one piece kneeling at the settee. At no time was I frightened, nor did the experience hurt. I had not been researching OBEs. I was amazed.'

CASESTUDY INDUCED OBE

One man first had an OBE as a child, then learned to induce the experiences: 'I was 12 years old when I had my first spontaneous OBE. The experience captivated me and around a year later I went out looking for a book on the subject. I found a small scientific study by a parapsychologist called Janet Lee Mitchell. I spent the next few months teaching myself how to induce the experience when my emotional state and level of relaxation were conducive enough. My first induced OBE was quite dramatic. I felt a pleasant surge of energy rush through my body, before becoming aware I was floating near the ceiling of my bedroom looking toward my bed below. I could just make out my body lying peacefully ... but it was the energy that seemed all around me and the vividness of my vision that

In summary

As the above examples highlight, OBEs can occur in a variety of contexts. Whether the OBEs discussed above took place during life-threatening or seemingly 'ordinary' circumstances, and whether they were intentionally induced or not, the OBErs clearly felt that they existed apart from their body and had lucid thought processes at the time their experience was occurring.

was really exciting to me. That experience seemed to open the flood gates and I have now had many experiences – journeys from one side of the globe to the other, and beyond. They have been hugely transformative – in a positive way ... Many of my OBEs have shown me things that appear to be objectively real, in much the same way as in NDE accounts.

'Soon after my first OBEs, I began to experiment with sensory deprivation, hypnosis, meditation, and different forms of technology including virtual reality. I began to explore ways to teach people to have their own experiences and I found that by making the methods for inducing OBEs specific to a person they became more effective ... what we eat, and how we work, learn, and inspire ourselves all have a tangible effect on developing the ability to enter the OBE.'

This whole chapter also shows us that, regardless of an NDE's specific nature, its after-effects are often long-lasting and life-changing. Whether for fear of being thought mad, or the impact of trauma, NDErs may take years just to develop the confidence to talk about their NDE. This naturally leads us to ask, then, whether all NDEs are essentially positive experiences (as are the ones presented in this chapter), or are many coloured by their distressing and unpleasant features?

CHAPTER 2
How distressing are NDEs?

In the early stages of research into NDE in the 1970s, NDErs consistently reported feeling pain-free, happy, ecstatic, joyful and tranquil – just like the case studies that we looked at in Chapter 1. Then, gradually, as more researchers delved deeper into the subject and gathered more stories, less pleasant experiences began to emerge. Nonetheless,

CASESTUDY DISTRESSING TO POSITIVE NDE

The life-review case study on page 28 was in fact a suicide attempt. Following her life review, the NDEr encountered sudden blackness and she felt as if she were suspended in outer space, an endless void with no light. She scanned around and saw a group of expressionless teenagers, whom she perceived to be 'other suicides'. Then with a sudden *whoosh!* an unidentified energy swept her away, at great speed, to a place that was 'charged with crackling energy'. She was surrounded by a fog-like mist that she surmised 'had mass – it seemed to be formed of molecules of intense darkness – and it could be handled and shaped. It had life ... some kind of intelligence that was purely negative, even evil.' Although she felt she was in 'hell', it wasn't the place of 'fire and brimstone' that she'd learned about as a child. She described it more like purgatory.

even today we have far fewer accounts of distressing experiences than of positive ones. Of course, we can't be certain why this is the case. While it might be because NDEs are generally more likely to be positive, it could also be that fewer NDErs with distressing experiences are willing to share their stories.

She could hear the 'buzz of thoughts' around her, of people trying to justify themselves, and saw others who were wearing dirty robes. She felt totally alone.

From a tiny pinpoint of light boomed a voice that said 'Is this what you really want?' and she knew that she was in the presence of God, made of light and glorious. She felt overwhelming love that 'had an entirely new dimension of pure compassion, of complete and perfect empathy'. She had a realization that her different choices could lead either to more despair or to new growth. She saw how the choice to end her life would not only affect others around her, but also potentially millions of people because we are all interconnected. The more light she experienced, the more it dissolved the darkness, and eventually it culminated in a rushing sensation that engulfed her body. The darkness sped past and she awoke in her body, her life transformed.

We may be inclined to overlook distressing types of NDE and focus on the stories that make us feel better, especially when it comes to considering death. I believe, though, that researchers have a responsibility to minimize how isolated distressing NDErs often feel, and should encourage them to share their accounts when they're ready.

Extremely distressing NDEs can leave some NDErs with a form of post-traumatic stress, which means it can be more damaging to force out their stories too early. However, that doesn't mean we should ignore them altogether: their eventual telling is fundamental to raising awareness of the true nature of the NDE, for making our research robust, and, of course, for helping these NDErs understand what happened to them, what it might mean, and how to integrate their experience positively in their lives.

Why are some NDEs distressing and others not?

We have no clear evidence why some people have pleasant NDEs and others have distressing ones. It would be logical to conclude that the circumstances of some cases could influence the experience. For example, we might think that a dangerous attack or attempted suicide – which are themselves fraught with negative emotions – lead to distressing NDEs. However, even when dangerous or distressing circumstances precede an NDE, there are many reports of the NDE itself being positive, or moving from distressing to positive (see case study, pages 38–9). Although in itself that doesn't prove that negative circumstances leading up to an NDE definitely don't cause distressing NDEs, it does show that, for now at least, until we have further research findings, there are no obvious answers as to why some NDEs are distressing and others aren't.

Some people have suggested that perhaps distressing NDEs are the province of NDErs who in life have been unkind or are morally flawed – but I've never found that to be consistently the case. Distressing NDEs are reported by the nicest, most loving, kind and caring people, too. (Equally, violent criminals seem just as likely to report pleasant NDEs.)

Another theory is that people who are used to being in control in their life are suddenly thrust into an overwhelming experience (in the form of an NDE) in which they try to maintain or regain control. Their attempts to resist what's happening (during the NDE) rather than surrender to it somehow upsets the balance of the experience, causing a sort of spiritual distress. There are many documented reports in which NDErs who relax during their NDE find they switch from an unpleasant to a pleasant experience.

Some researchers have suggested that NDErs with repressed guilt, or residual fear and anger in life, and those who expect punishment or judgement at death, are more likely to have a distressing NDE. However, I think we all have repressed emotions or guilt at some level, so I don't think this provides a full enough explanation as to why some NDEs are distressing and others are not.

Finally, there is the possibility of the influence of the individual's religious upbringing. Could images of fire and brimstone, for example, impact on how certain people interpret their NDE? Could some people simply be fearful because they have previously declared themselves to be an atheist? Or could the problem be one merely of interpretation: we expect flames to depict hell and horror, so we interpret them in that way? Could it be that, in fact, those flames represent strength or regeneration, like the phoenix rising from the ashes? And is it therefore all a matter of personal associations and interpretations?

Are there common features of a distressing NDE?

My 20 years of research have given me quite a few accounts of distressing NDEs. The commonality between them is that they seem to be a much more sensitive type of experience than positive NDEs and, unless recounted straightaway consistently take longer to understand in any depth. Of

CASESTUDIES TWO FRIGHTENING NDEs

In the first account of a distressing NDE I ever heard, the woman described leaving her body and looking down at herself sitting in the chair. She felt herself floating toward a big bridge with a river running underneath it. She was afraid of water, and as she got closer to the bridge – and so the river – she became more afraid. As her anxiety increased she could hear children's voices in the background and it felt as though these voices were mocking her. She was convinced she was dead.

In the second account, the NDEr described seeing a lady with a straw hat on her head sitting in a rowing boat on a lake. The NDEr giving the account didn't recognize the lady, but knew she should stay away from her. Then, she saw a round wheel, lit up with vivid colours. These colours had heat coming from them and 'horrible smoke'. The NDEr felt as though she were looking into 'hell' and could feel heat from 'the flames of hell'. I had to terminate this interview because recounting the NDE became distressing for her – so much so, in fact, that she refused to discuss it with me again, even a few days later.

course, this isn't that surprising – it takes time to come to terms with any traumatic experience (even one that happens while we're healthy, in our everyday course of existence). As our mind processes trauma, we often actively avoid trying to remember and recount it. We bring the traumatic experience back in manageable chunks, little by little, giving us time to remember and adjust. When it comes to distressing NDEs, the NDErs are more likely than others to feel isolated by or afraid of their experience (remember, most published accounts of NDE tend to be of positive experiences), extending the time it takes before they are willing to talk, and, in turn, slowing down the healing process.

Another prominent researcher who has explored distressing NDEs in depth is Nancy Evans Bush, author of the book *Dancing Past the Dark*. She herself had a distressing NDE (see case study, opposite) that sparked her initial interest in exploring this topic.

Along with her colleague Professor Bruce Greyson, Nancy Evans spent the years between 1982 and 1992 gathering and analyzing many examples of distressing NDEs. The researchers came up with three categories of distressing NDE, which can either stand alone or appear in combination with one another (these are discussed on pages 46–7).

CASESTUDY DISTRESSING NDE IN CHILDBIRTH

During a complicated experience of childbirth,
Nancy Evans Bush (see opposite) suddenly felt herself
travelling extremely fast through space, covering a
vast distance. Ahead of her a group of circles, each
coloured black and white, appeared. The colours of
the circles weren't static – they continually alternated
from black to white and back again, making a clicking
sound as they did so. They seemed to be giving Nancy
a message that her life had never existed and that
she'd been allowed to make it up: there was nothing
there and she was not real. Nancy didn't speak about
her experience at the time, because she couldn't find a
way to understand what it meant.

Many years later, Nancy picked up a book on Eastern
philosophy at a friend's house and instantly recognized
the Chinese symbol of yin–yang, which represents
the unity of opposites. Overcome with emotion, she
realized this was the origin of the black-and-white
circles she'd seen during her NDE. The NDE and her
realization had such a profound effect on her that
she went on to dedicate her life to improving our
understanding of distressing NDEs.

1. The typical NDE interpreted in a distressing way
Featuring many of the usual components of the NDE (see page 21), this category is distressing because the experience itself *feels* unpleasant. The NDE provokes anxiety in the experiencer and no feelings of peace, tranquillity or joy. The first example on page 43 is good for this category.

2. The void experience
In this category the NDEr feels that he or she has been plunged into a dark, meaningless, eternal void. Many NDErs have described it as an experience of 'nothingness'. Sometimes they can hear mocking voices saying that life is just a joke. Nancy Bush's experience (see case study, page 45) is a good example of a void experience.

3. The hell-like experience
The most frightening type of distressing NDE, hell-like NDEs were first described in 1979 by cardiologist Dr Maurice Rawlings. While performing a 'stress test' on a 48-year-old male patient, the patient's heart stopped beating and he slumped to the floor. Rawlings and the nurses with him began resuscitating the patient and inserted a pacemaker into the man's heart. At several points during the procedure, the patient came round, then lost consciousness again. Each time he regained consciousness, he screamed that he was in hell. He begged Rawlings and the nurses not to stop their

attempts to resuscitate him, because every time they did so, he was plunged back into hell.

A few days later Rawlings visited the patient with the intention of asking him about what he recalled of his resuscitation experience. However, the patient had no recall at all. Rawlings believes that this is because the experience was so utterly traumatic that the patient's brain suppressed it, perhaps indefinitely.

In the interests of objectivity, it's important to say that this account is not without its critics: Rawlings was deeply religious and others claimed his interpretation was heavily influenced by his own religious views. In fact, Rawlings himself admitted this was probably the case. Nonetheless, the account of a hell-like experience concurs with the categories set out by Nancy Evans Bush and Bruce Greyson, who later found other examples of the 'hellish' experience.

Other findings about distressing NDEs
Late cardiologist Dr Barbara Rommer gathered more than 300 cases of NDEs in the USA, nearly 18 per cent of which were of the distressing kind. She agreed with Bush and Greyson's three categories, and added one more: a category of distressing NDE in which the life review was in itself traumatic. Some of her research subjects found

themselves in the disturbing situation of appearing before a tribunal or being judged by a higher power.

British researcher Dr Margot Grey also acknowledged distressing NDEs. She categorized them in only two ways – negative and hell-like. In her research negative experiences included fear, extreme panic, mental anguish, desperation, and feelings of being lost, helpless and lonely. The environment for these NDEs was barren, hostile, dark and gloomy. Sometimes the NDEr described looking into a pit or being on the edge of an abyss.

Dr Grey's hell-like experience was an intensified version of the negative experience and included imagery of faceless or hooded beings, a sense of an evil force, as well as demonic creatures, wailing souls, noises of wild beasts, an encounter with the devil and extreme feelings of hot or cold. Some of these components form part of the NDE described in the case study on pages 38–9.

Can people experience both pleasant and distressing NDEs at the same time?

Some research shows that NDEs may begin as pleasant but turn into something distressing. Conversely, as in the case study below, some NDEs have started off as distressing and then turned pleasant.

CASESTUDY A DISTRESSING NDE THAT BECAME PLEASANT

In 2010, Dr Rajiv Parti, an anaesthesiologist practising in California, had a hellish NDE during a complicated and life-threatening surgery. He described foreboding imagery of thunder and lightning storms, and black clouds. He could see people being tortured and feel people sticking needles into him. He could smell burning flesh. Then, he had a sudden insight into the way he was living his life – he realized he had been very selfish and unforgiving. As soon as he had this insight, the whole NDE completely changed – hellfire and darkness disappeared and were replaced with images of great beauty and a deep sense of pure love.

How common are distressing NDEs versus pleasant ones?

Distressing NDEs are not uncommon – and if you've had one you are certainly not alone. As part of my work, I'm trying to develop therapeutic interventions to help anyone who has had a distressing NDE to understand and integrate the experience into his or her life. It's so important that you come forward to share your story, when you're ready.

FOCUS ON USING NDEs AS MORAL GUIDES

In ancient literature, distressing imagery and descriptions of unpleasant encounters are often associated with death, and these seem to have had a practical use in helping people navigate this inevitability. Texts such as *The Tibetan Book of the Dead,* for example, where death is described as having the appearance of terrifying wrathful deities, were recited over the bodies of dying people with the intention of guiding them through death.

According to Professor Carol Zaleski in her book *Otherworld Journeys: Accounts of Near-death Experience in Medieval and Modern Times,* descriptions of NDEs appear throughout medieval literature, to warn others away from immoral lifestyles that would prevent them from reaching the Otherworld. Journeys to the Otherworld are described as dark, thorny paths full of obstacles, such as slippery bridges, rivers of fire or sharp knives. Safe passage depended on good deeds performed during life. These accounts show how NDEs could inspire transformation when the NDErs returned to life, with many relinquishing their possessions and living ascetically.

At present, differences in research methodologies, and sample sizes and types mean there are no definitive statistics about the numbers of distressing NDEs versus pleasant ones. However, estimates are that between 14 and 18 per cent of all NDEs fall into the distressing category. We hope that statistics should prove increasingly useful and conclusive as more research studies are done.

Are there negative after-effects of distressing NDEs?

The reverberations of many distressing NDEs can often be quite traumatic, leaving the individual with a sense of guilt, shame or stigma. Many people are left feeling isolated, not knowing where to turn for help. It is extremely difficult to get people who have had a distressing NDE to disclose their experience, particularly as time passes. In the course of my research I've definitely had more success gaining insight into negative experiences with NDErs whom I've interviewed soon after their NDE, for example while they are still in hospital, than with those who have emailed me long after the NDE happened. I have found that once I begin an email conversation with someone, it can take months to get even the briefest of details about a distressing NDE. In quite a few cases NDErs tend to shy away or back off completely once they are at the point of recounting a certain detail of their distressing experience. Other researchers, including Nancy Evans Bush (see page 44), report similar findings.

It could be that, over time, distressed NDErs repress or internalize specific, detailed memories of the event in order to avoid bringing their trauma into the present day. Many are left with questions such as 'Why did I have a bad experience?' or 'Am I a bad person because I went to hell?' Feeling unable to discuss the experience at the time it happens alienates these experiencers and exacerbates the effects of the distressing NDE in the long term. Nancy Bush noted three main reactions to the distressing NDE experience:

1. **A conversion response**
In this response, people come out of the experience to change their lives for the better.

2 **A reductionist response**
This tries to rationalize the experience by saying that it was all the result of the release of endorphins (chemical messengers in the brain), or of a neurological event.

3 **The onset of a long-standing struggle**
A person may spend a long time trying to understand the experience and suffer from a continued fear of death (appropriate therapy to recognize the distressing NDE and the person's reaction to it is particularly helpful in these circumstances).

Can distressing NDEs have positive effects?

Some research studies show that many people who experience distressing NDEs have interpreted them as a warning – a wake-up call that has then motivated them to modify their real-life behaviour and attitude. In some cases this has been because the NDE provided them with a sign that there is life after death. Some researchers found, interestingly, that those who had a distressing NDE were able to integrate the experience into their life much quicker than those who had a pleasant experience. This is in contrast to other findings (see opposite), but could be explained as the NDEr being inspired to re-evaluate their behaviour and change the way they lived their life, with the recollection of their distressing NDE serving as a constant reminder for making better lifestyle choices.

How can we help those who've had distressing NDEs?

In the initial aftermath of a distressing NDE, just talking about the experience with someone who is likely to understand – such as another NDEr, a therapist familiar with NDEs, or a support group specializing in the phenomena – can help. The purpose of support groups is to provide a safe place for anyone who has had an NDE, whether positive or distressing, to share their experience in a safe environment surrounded by people who truly understand what an NDE feels like.

Researcher Nancy Evans Bush has suggested ways to help NDErs in a palliative-care setting who, following their NDE become afraid to face impending death. First, she suggests we simply listen, and then explain that throughout history, ordinary people as well as religious ascetics have had experiences akin to what we now call NDEs. We should explain that these accounts reassure us that while a spiritual experience can sometimes be distressing to start with, it may become pleasant. Then, we should go on to describe some pleasant NDEs. Importantly, she advises reframing the NDErs' experiences so that any demons can be seen as guides and any punishment can be re-evaluated as a form of purification. She stresses the importance of telling NDErs that should a similar experience happen again, they should look for and ask for the light while they are within the NDE itself.

Recounting the distressing NDEs of other people, and explaining how they can be a trigger for positive change is another important way in which we can help those who have had a distressing NDE. The case study of the woman who had tried to commit suicide, whose visions of a hell-like world became a world infused with peace and love that had long-lasting positive effects on her real life is a good example (see case study, pages 38–9). She realized that while hell is a dimension (a place where her NDE was partly played out), it is primarily a state of mind. She understood that she'd been living in hell, saying after the event: 'When we die our state of mind grows far more obvious because we are gathered with those who think as we do.' She was referring to the other, expressionless spirits she'd encountered while in her NDE. Before re-entering her body she understood how important her life was and was overwhelmed with a sense of gratitude – which was exactly what she needed to effect life change.

It's also worth exploring the possibility that a distressing NDE that didn't have a positive ending may have been cut short. As supportive onlookers, we can work with NDErs to explore how any positive components in their distressing NDEs may have played out if the experiences had been seen through all the way to a pleasant conclusion.

CHAPTER 3

Who has NDEs and under what circumstances do they occur?

Research shows that anyone can have an NDE – people from all walks of life, culture, professions, geographical regions, and educational backgrounds. Among famous people to have had them are the actors Peter Sellers, Larry Hagman, Elizabeth Taylor, Jane Seymour and Sharon Stone (see below). While cultural beliefs may inform specific content, the same themes of NDEs exist throughout the world.

CASESTUDY **SHARON STONE'S STORY**

In an interview with US talk-show host Oprah Winfrey in 2004, the movie actress Sharon Stone described her own NDE, which had occurred around three years previously when she had a bleed on her brain. After her MRI scan, she was surrounded by doctors whom she describes as looking at her calmly and sympathetically. She experienced what she refers to as a 'big blow up'. She not only saw a white light, but had people who had died talk to her. Her overwhelming sensation was that death was near, but that it was a safe, loving, gentle place and not scary. She had realized that she'd been dead, but also that she'd had a choice to come back to life. She wanted to live, to be with her son, so she chose to come back.

Can young children have NDEs?

Children of any age can have NDEs, and most children who do so simply accept their NDEs as a normal part of life (with the sense that everyone has them). Even young children – who may have no concept of death – have reported what we know to be NDEs. The experiences of these young children are particularly interesting – some describe situations in which they see relatives who died before they were born. Four-year-old Colton Burpo, for example, had an NDE in which he watched the doctor operate on him in theatre. During his NDE he encountered his dead grandfather – a man who had died 34 years earlier, long before Colton was born. Even more intriguing is that Colton told his parents he'd been talking to his other sister, the one who had 'died in (their mother's) tummy'. Colton's mother had indeed miscarried a baby, but no one had ever told the young boy about it. Colton's father, Todd, wrote a book, *Heaven is for Real* (now also a Hollywood movie) about his son's experience.

Are the NDEs of children identical to those of adults?

Some researchers found that the life review (see page 28) is less common in childhood NDEs. Given that children have less life experience to reflect on, this wouldn't be that surprising. However, later research has contradicted this finding, which could lead to the conclusion that length of life does not influence if a person will have a life review or not.

CASESTUDY **A FIVE-YEAR-OLD'S NDE**

I met Francesca, a young woman, in London in 2015.
She told me about the NDE she'd had when she was
five years old. It provides a good example of how a
childhood NDE can have a long-term effect: 'I was in
an inflatable dinghy in a swimming pool and I fell in.
I couldn't swim and I remember struggling a bit and
then seeing my body as if it were somebody else's –
but knowing it was mine. I remember seeing my long,
curly hair fanned out in the water, sunshine, and a
green light, and feeling absolutely calm and peaceful.
I remember giving the green light my full attention
and really wanting to follow it, but then waking up to
my dad who had jumped in to save me. Incidentally,
he had a very similar experience when he was young,
but actually went through a dark tunnel and his great
grandma told him not to come any closer.

'I had forgotten about my experience until I read an
account of an NDE shortly before I started a SCUBA-
diving course. Learning to dive was quite traumatic
for me at first. Then I realized there was nothing to be
scared of and that same delicious feeling of tranquillity
came back to me.'

While adult NDErs usually see dead people, children also report seeing relatives who are still alive, perhaps because they have less first-hand knowledge of death in their young lives than adults. Finally, seeing dead pets seems to be more common in childhood NDEs, although I've had accounts of adult NDEs that include dead pets, too.

How do NDEs affect children's lives in the future?
Different researchers report different levels and types of after-effects among children who've had an NDE. Some young people later report that they've had a deep-held longing to return to the beautiful place of their NDE. A child may even become depressed because he or she can't revisit the scene of the NDE.

Some researchers have reported cases in which child NDErs have developed a greater desire for learning and knowledge. One study of 20 children showed that those who'd had an NDE displayed highly developed artistic abilities or showed a keen desire to meditate. On the other hand, other NDE children can be more introverted or disruptive. Of course, small samples can't necessarily provide convincing evidence, but they do show that it would be worth pursuing these threads in the future with more research and greater sample sizes.

Dr Melvin Morse, a US paediatrician with a specialism in NDEs, re-interviewed 30 of his research-group subjects to find that the children had grown up to become well-balanced, well-rounded young people (for example, they had not turned to drugs or alcohol). However, US NDE researcher P M H Atwater found that a third of her study group of childhood NDErs went on to abuse alcohol. Why the different findings? It could be that the two research studies used different methodologies, giving them incomparable results. Or, it could be that Morse's study validated the NDEs for the children just as they were beginning to understand what had happened to them, resulting in long-term benefits. Atwater's study, on the other hand, was conducted retrospectively, which meant that she didn't have the chance to validate the experiences for the children close to the time they occurred.

Do NDEs occur in populations all over the world?

There have been numerous reports of NDEs from places across the globe. The biggest online collection of NDEs is on the website for the Near Death Experience Research Foundation (NDERF). Set up by US NDE researcher Dr Jeffrey Long and his wife Jody, the site includes NDE reports from all cultures in all countries. The differences and similarities between these international experiences are incredibly important to the study of NDEs.

What sorts of NDEs do other culture groups describe?

Although NDEs all over the world show major similarities, there are also cultural differences that consistently occur in NDErs' accounts. For example, in Hindu culture, the life review that many western NDErs report may be replaced with an encounter with Chitragupta, the Hindu god who keeps a record of human deeds, and decides the fate of the dead.

Before we go any further down this path, however, I want to point out that there hasn't yet been a full multicultural analysis of NDEs. While my own research hints at some cultural similarities and differences in NDEs, these may not be truly representative of a whole culture in general.

Reports from NDErs living in western societies, such as the UK, USA, Europe and Australia, tend to follow the same set of fundamental characteristics – those I set out in Chapter 1 (see page 21). However, not all NDEs within a single geographical region follow the same pattern, if the region includes distinct cultural differences. For example, westernized Australian NDE accounts tend to show different characteristics from those of the Australian Aborigines.

NDEs among the Australian Aborigines

We have very few historical, written accounts of NDEs among the Aborigines – this is because the Aborigines have an oral tradition whereby experiences are passed on by word of mouth. Without written accounts to compare, finding threads of similarity is all the more difficult. One account, though, relates a man who described his NDE as a canoe ride to the land of the dead. Here, he met his deceased relatives, along with the Turtle Man Spirit. This and other spirits gave him gifts and danced for him, then sent him back to life, promising him he could return when he died.

NDEs among the Maori of New Zealand

The Maoris also rely upon oral accounts. One case tells of a lady whom everyone believed was dead. Plans for her funeral had been made, but as her relatives grieved around her, she came back to life. During the time she appeared to be dead, she had left her body and travelled across various New Zealand landmarks to the place where spirits leap off a ledge into the Underworld. She looked from the ledge to the subterranean passage below, the entrance to the Underworld itself. She had undertaken some rituals required of the dead and was about to embark upon her own leap when a voice told her to go back. The voice told her it wasn't her time and that she'd be recalled to the ledge in the future.

NDEs in Hawaii, Guam, Chile and Melanesia

Early accounts from Hawaii, Guam and the Mapuche people of Chile also describe out-of-body travel, walking along paths, sometimes toward a volcano, meeting deceased relatives, encountering a barrier and being sent back to life (many of which have similarities with western NDE characteristics; see page 21). NDErs report watching scenes of others being judged and punished during their experiences, identifying those others as sorcerers. Descriptions of deceased relatives, religious figures and a white-robed, bearded man also came up in the accounts, but the OBE, tunnel and feelings of peace and joy did not. Interestingly, the few cases that were reported from Melanesia had scenes of industrialization and motorways instead of beautiful gardens.

NDEs in the Philippines

More recent cases from the Philippines were reported to me by former colleagues between 2004 and 2010. These were similar to accounts from the West. They included OBE travel and attempts to communicate with bystanders, travelling toward or trying to reach a bright light, and hearing a voice or sensing a presence. Some accounts relayed a strenuous attempt to get to the light or an arduous journey to the top of a mountain to be greeted by a bearded man wearing a long white robe, before finally being sent back to life.

NDEs in Hindu culture

Many Indian accounts of NDE omit the tunnel component that often appears in western versions of the experience.

NDErs may be led away to the Underworld by yamdoots (messengers of Yama, the god of the dead) to meet deceased relatives and religious figures. In Hindu culture, the life review is reported as a sequence of events read aloud from or documented in a book. Some NDErs have claimed that the realization of a clerical error highlights the fact that he or she is the wrong person for the Underworld realm at this time – and that's why he or she is sent back to life.

NDEs in Thailand

There are only a small number of published accounts of Thai NDEs. Buddhist themes – with an emphasis on good deeds (such as compassion and generosity) that the NDEr has accrued during his or her life – feature heavily. Some NDErs report that accountants read from the book of accounts, while Yama decides the NDEr's fate. Yama's messengers (see above) also appear consistently among Thai accounts. Unsurprisingly, perhaps, given the strong Buddhist influence in Thailand, China and parts of India, NDE accounts show similarities across these nations.

NDEs in Japan

Themes of Japanese NDEs include OBE travel over fields of beautiful flowers, feelings of peace, rivers, time distortion, ght golden light, and meeting deceased relatives who s   the experiencer back to life. One Japanese researcher also reported some cases of distressing NDEs, including themes of pain, fear and suffering.

NDEs in China

Monks who recovered from life-threatening illnesses give China some of its earliest accounts of NDEs. One such case describes the monk entering a void and having a light put into his hand. Others describe the NDEr emerging from a dark tubular structure, a review of sinful deeds, beings of light, and beautiful environments. Later research into the NDE experiences of survivors of the Tangshan earthquake (in 1976), as well as even more recent accounts, describe some of the characteristics common to western NDEs (see page 21).

NDEs in Africa

Many African accounts of NDEs involve people dressed in white robes, encountering a barrier and being sent back to life. One case described the NDEr calling out to Jesus for help – in response, obstacles moved from his path during the NDE. Another NDEr found himself standing before a man holding a book. As the man looked at the names in the book, it became clear that the name of the NDEr was not there. The man told him it was not his time and sent him back to life. In another account the NDEr describes a journey along a path. When he comes to a fork in the path, he is unsure which route to take. Two men appear – one tries to lead him along the path to hell, but the other rescues him and he revives.

NDEs in Islamic countries

Themes from Muslim NDE accounts include OBEs (in particular, watching the resuscitation from above), travel through a tunnel toward a bright light, a panoramic life review, meeting a religious figure and dead relatives, non-verbal communication with the deceased, and being sent back to life. In other words, non-western Muslim NDEs show striking similarities with westerners' NDEs.

NDEs in Native American culture

OBE travel, trying to communicate with people who are still alive, entering a cavern-like entrance, hearing voices, being with guides or spirits and being sent back to life to tell others how to live wisely are common Native American NDE themes.

NDEs in the rest of the world

It's not possible in a relatively small book like this one to cover every scenario in every culture – we've looked only at a brief overview that is no way exhaustive. In some cultures spiritual practices enable highly skilled practitioners to induce a journey to the realm of spirits in which they believe. In Tibet there are individuals, usually women, who are so extremely disciplined in their spiritual practice that they are able to induce a state in which their heartbeat is undetectable, making them appear to be dead to others. These 'delogs', as they are known, can stay in a state of apparent absence of vital signs for days. They describe that while they are in this state, they are able to leave their body and travel to the Underworld to witness the torture of sinners. Visible to the Underworld spirits, the delogs are asked to give messages to the spirits' living family members and to perform rituals that will absolve their sins. During the NDE the delogs often meet their own deceased relatives and go to a paradise-like realm.

In summary

What this brief culture-by-culture overview shows us is that every NDE is deeply embedded in its own cultural heritage. Czech psychiatrist Dr Stanislav Grof, one of the founding fathers of transpersonal psychology, who has undertaken pioneering work into altered states of consciousness, believes that these experiences are maps of the human psyche. What he means is that an NDE connects us to a certain place and belief system – when we have an NDE, elements of the actual experience, as well as our interpretation of it, reflect the belief systems of the world in which we have grown up and lived. He also believes that the psyche reveals we are all interconnected, that it breaks down cultural boundaries.

Do NDEs happen only at 'clinical' death?

There is a significant misconception, even among the medical profession, that a person has to be clinically dead to experience an NDE. This is not the case. NDEs can also occur during life-threatening circumstances (such as on pages 22–23) – the person's heart does not necessarily have to have stopped beating. However, my hospital research shows me that NDEs are more likely to occur in people who have, in fact, been clinically dead – such as those who have undergone a cardiac arrest and been successfully resuscitated.

NDEs and cardiac arrest

US cardiologist Dr Michael Sabom, who undertook hospital research in the 1980s, reported many cases of NDEs during cardiac arrest. Further research by others supports the notion that cardiac arrest can be a trigger for NDEs. According to the hospital studies, the frequency of NDEs in patients who survive cardiac arrest is between 11 and 23 per cent.

In the first year of my own hospital research, I interviewed every patient who survived their admission to the intensive care unit (ITU). Not all these patients came close to death, but I wanted to see exactly how common NDEs were and which, if any, illnesses were more likely to yield such an experience. After the first year not many people reported an NDE – less than 1 per cent of the total sample, in fact. However, when I modified the research and looked at only survivors of cardiac arrest, I found that the frequency of NDEs increased to nearly 18 per cent.

Further investigation into OBEs
More hospital research is needed into OBEs that occur during NDEs. Recent research has entailed placing targets around areas of the room where resuscitation is likely to take place. A patient would be able to see the targets only from the perspective of an OBE. If an NDEr later identifies the targets, we know that what the NDEr sees during an OBE is 'real' rather than imagined. Examining the medical notes documenting the circumstances of a patient's admission, and interviewing staff who are there while a patient is resuscitated provides context so that we can build a picture of what medical circumstances might lead to OBE during NDE. The medical notes for each NDEr can show us how close the person comes to death, how long he or she is unconscious, what treatment he or she receives and any blood results.

CASESTUDY EMERGENCY CHILDBIRTH NDE

One woman recounted the NDE that occurred while she was in labour: 'I received my epidural at 1:50 am. At 2:00 am I blanked out. What I felt was like a vivid dream: I was rushing through what seemed like a kaleidoscope, with images of my life and family and friends appearing in front of me. Then, I was rushing backward and the next thing I knew I was very disappointed to wake up with doctors and nurses trying to get me to respond. I remember asking why did they wake me when I was having a wonderful dream? I wanted to go back to sleep, but I knew I needed to deliver my baby. I turned to see my husband crying; he thought I'd died.

'They were very concerned about me and monitored me closely for days. However, no one ever explained to me why it happened. All I know is that my blood pressure plunged. It was a very vivid experience ... I wondered if I'd had an NDE?'

What other circumstances can lead to NDEs?

NDEs can occur in all sorts of situations and close brushes with death, including near-drowning, during surgical procedures, during car accidents, and during suicide attempts. Early on in my study of NDEs, I began to realize that NDEs seem to occur with relative frequency during two particular circumstances. The first circumstance occurs among women who have had emergency or complicated childbirth experiences (see case study, opposite), and the second occurs among children who have had gas to anaesthetize them during a tooth extraction (see case study, overleaf).

Are NDEs a phenomenon of modern times?

Evidence suggests that NDEs have occurred since time immemorial. There are many accounts of experiences we might now refer to as NDEs in ancient literature. *Otherworld Journeys* by Professor Carol Zaloski (discussed in the box on page 50) is one of the most extensive collections of such historical cases.

Do only religious people have NDEs?

NDEs do not seem to be limited to those who follow any particular kind of spirituality – whether that's an organized religion or a non-secular belief in otherworldly powers. Former Professor of Art and confessed atheist Howard Storm experienced an NDE when he became gravely ill as a result of a perforated stomach. His experience had such an impact on his life that his religious beliefs were completely transformed afterwards– he resigned from his job and devoted his life to attending the United Theological Seminary, becoming a minister for the United Church of Christ. Another example of an NDEr subsequently embracing religion can be seen in the case study on page 76.

The British philosopher and atheist A J Ayer (1910–1989) also had an NDE. Having been discharged from hospital following a bout of pneumonia, Ayer had a relapse. Back in hospital, as he was making a recovery, he nearly choked on some smoked salmon. Cardiograms show that his heart rate plummeted, and we know that the ward sister rushed

---

CASESTUDY **NDE DURING TOOTH EXTRACTION**

One man told me the following account from his childhood: 'I had an NDE as a child at the dentist. I had to have some teeth out by gas ... The mask was put over my mouth and the smell of rubber was horrendous ... But soon I was asleep. I remember I was floating on a grey blanket above myself and seeing my mum watching the dentist from the chair in the corner of the room ... I then floated out of the room and down the stairs, but before getting to the bottom I awoke ... I was so ill that the dentist's nurse had to take my mum and me home in her car – I could not even stand up ...'

---

to attend to him: his heart had stopped for four minutes. Although he had no recollection of the physical events from the point at which he passed out as a result of the choking until he came round in the ITU, he did recall one vivid memory.

He wrote about it in an article for the *Sunday Telegraph* on August 28, 1988. He described being confronted by a very bright, red light, which he believed was responsible for the government of the universe. Within the light were two creatures responsible for space. A space inspection revealed that these creatures had been unsuccessful in their work and space was out of joint. Ayer felt it was up to him to rectify the situation. His article reads: 'It then occurred to me that whereas, until the present century, physicists accepted the Newtonian severance of space and time, it had become customary since the vindication of Einstein's general theory of relativity, to treat space−time as a single whole. Accordingly, I thought I could cure space by operating upon time.'

He concluded that 'death does not put an end to consciousness ... My recent experiences have slightly weakened my conviction that my genuine death, which is due fairly soon, will be the end of me, though I continue to hope that it will be. They have not weakened my conviction that there is no God.' However, almost six months later

Ayer wrote a further article in *The Spectator*, retracting his
dismissiveness of God: 'What I should have said, had I not
been anxious to appear undogmatic, is that my experiences
have weakened, not my belief that there is no life after death,
but my inflexible attitude toward that belief.'

These examples of formerly non-religious people finding
new spiritual beliefs following an NDE show the profoundly
transformative effects this phenomenon can have. It
therefore stands to reason that NDEs can have profound
effects on a person's life after the experience. We will
explore this topic in the next chapter.

CHAPTER 4

What are the life-changing
effects of NDEs?

Research shows us that the effects of experiencing an NDE occur on many levels – physical and psychological, as well as spiritual. An NDE may completely 'reset' a person's consciousness, having come close to death, or having seen what it means to teeter on the brink between life and death, NDErs often feel reborn with a completely new attitude to living and a new appreciation for, and understanding, of life.

What psychological changes commonly occur?

Of course, not all psychological changes present themselves in every person who has had an NDE, but the following are those that occur most commonly:

- Lessened fear of death
- Changed attitude toward others
- Redressed sense of value
- Need to simplify life or career
- Greater self-belief

Lessened fear of death

Probably the most common and most profound effect of an NDE is to transform how the person views death. Most people who have had a pleasant NDE report coming away with a deep-seated conviction that death is nothing to fear – the majority feel that they've already been through death and that it was wonderful. In some instances feeling comfortable with the notion of death itself goes hand in hand with a new and strong conviction that there is life after death. Research shows that, of course, not all people become totally fearless at the prospect of facing their mortality. Some seem to have only a minimal reduction in fear; others come away with no new impression of what it means to die at all. In my own hospital research, I found that the depth of the NDE was a determining factor in how profoundly someone's views about death changed once he or she returned to life.

In my studies those whose NDE had fewer of Moody's defining characteristics (see page 21) seemed to have experienced a less significant reduction in their fears about death. Those who'd experienced more of those characteristics had a greater reduction. Of all my subjects the two who'd had the deepest NDEs with the most defining characteristics had become adamant that death was nothing to fear at all.

One ward patient, who'd had an NDE during a cardiac arrest, was almost euphoric about his experience. He wanted to share it with everyone, visiting other critically ill patients to tell them that they had no need to be afraid of death, that death was wonderful. Another hospital patient visited each bedside in his rehabilitation centre to describe his NDE and encourage other patients not to fear death. His positivity changed the mood of his ward – patients who had previously not been motivated to get out of bed or get dressed were now up and about, in their chairs, wearing day clothes instead of pyjamas. His own transformational experience had a ripple effect on those around him – and their families, many of whom wrote to him afterwards to thank him for his help.

Changed attitude toward others

While the effects of NDEs may seem life- (and death-) affirming, in fact many NDErs begin to wonder if their life before their NDE was meaningless. Such a realization can increase feelings of isolation – how can you share with your loved ones the notion that you think your life with them before your experience was unfulfilling? As a knock-on effect, some NDErs report feeling frustrated that those who were once close to them now have no real understanding of what's happened; some even say they feel their experience is treated with dismissiveness, making them feel shunned by their loved ones. The natural result of this is that people grow apart – divorce, for example, is a relatively common result when one member of a couple has experienced an NDE.

On the other hand, many NDErs become more tolerant, loving, empathic and compassionate toward others. Some may find a new sense of selflessness – the NDEr no longer feels the centre of his or her own life, but sees that we are each a part of a much greater, interconnected whole.

Many of the NDErs I've interviewed or have read about have wanted to devote their lives following their NDE to the service of others. Some often feel a calling to be with people as they are dying and undertake hospice work or go on to train to be nurses or 'soul midwives' (see box, page 131).

Redressed sense of value

Many NDErs report thinking about material possessions in a new way. Status symbols, such as a big house, the latest gadgets or a flash car, lose their meaning. Instead, NDErs feel new appreciation for things that have spiritual or emotional rather than material value, such as spending quality time with loved ones or reconnecting with nature (many of my subjects reported finding a new love of long countryside walks, or strolling along beaches or appreciating the beauty of trees).

Need to simplify life or career

After an NDE, a greater sense of compassion and reduced need for material possessions may combine to motivate many NDErs to give up high-flying careers with their accompanying large salaries and high stress levels. Instead they may want to do something more worthwhile or for the good of others (such as becoming a nurse or 'soul midwife'), perhaps even on a volunteer basis. I discovered that those who did return to their former careers tended to do so at reduced hours or with less responsibility.

Greater self-belief

The overwhelming feelings of well-being that some people have following an NDE seem to boost their faith in their ability to perform great feats. One of my subjects became so certain of her ability to push her physical body to its limits, she became an ultra-distance runner – appearing in the book of *Guinness World Records* three times!

What changes might occur in spiritual outlook?

These are the spiritual changes most often reported following an NDE:

- Realigning spiritual values
- Finding a mission or purpose in life
- Discovering the interconnectivity of all things

Realigning spiritual values

In Chapter 3 we looked at how even those who have no religion, or actively shunned secular religion, may have a spiritual transformation as a result of having an NDE (see pages 73–6). These people subsequently adopted a belief in God or higher power, and perhaps attended church for the first time or more frequently after their NDE. Interestingly, some people report having been very religious before their NDE, but experiencing diminishing faith following it. In these cases the reason for loss of faith tends to be that the teachings of the particular religion do not compare with the overwhelming spiritual experience of the NDE. These NDErs may turn to a more non-secular spirituality.

Finding a mission or purpose in life

Coming back to life for many NDErs seems to trigger a renewed sense of purpose in life or a mission that they need to fulfil. This might be as straightforward as a need to share with as many people as possible the retelling of the NDE (this also helps the NDEr come to terms with the NDE); while others may feel they are unable to remember or identify exactly what their new purpose or mission is. There are many psychological and emotional responses to this, not least a sense of being lost. Still others might have a clear purpose to 'do good'.

Discovering the interconnectivity of all things

The life-review feature of an NDE (see case study, page 28) particularly highlights the interconnectivity of all things. Many NDErs realize that every action has an impact on other people, and on the world. This new sense of being part of a whole can lead to renewed purpose or greater empathy.

As mentioned on page 83, some NDErs also report feeling more connected to nature than they had done previously. With an expanded world view, a sense of their blinkers being removed enables the NDEr to see the impact of their actions, and the actions of all of humanity, have on the environment (see page 125).

What sort of physical changes occur after NDEs?

NDEs are such overtly spiritual and psychological experiences, it can be easy to overlook their physical effects. Of course, some people have to deal with physical injuries

---

CASESTUDY **FINDING PURPOSE**

Founder of the Love, Care, Share Foundation (see below), Kelly Walsh came to me with a profound experience that was not strictly an NDE, as she was not under threat of death at the time, but rather a spiritually transformative experience (STE). She had attempted suicide, but was discovered in time to bring her back to life. Admitted to a psychiatric ward, that night she 'had the sensation of travelling through what felt like bumps in the universe, while elements of my life were played out in front of me. This journey at times was unpleasant and it actually felt like a battle or test. I went through seven bumps in total and then all of a sudden the battle was over and I was enveloped by unconditional love. In the void I heard a voice that said I was strong and

sustained at the time of the NDE (for example, if they were in an accident). However, the physical changes I'm talking about here are more anomalous: we don't always understand how they could have happened, nor how quickly. For example, some NDErs seem to develop a reduced tolerance to pharmaceutical drugs, or to alcohol or other chemicals; others report remarkable, seemingly miraculous, healing.

I had a mission to carry out. It was demonstrated to me that we are all one, all connected and that through love the world can heal. Self-love being the most important love of all. I came around from the experience with my arms across my chest and opened them in slow motion like a rebirth. The following evening I shouted out that like-minded souls would collaborate to change the world.' Inspired by her experience, Kelly set up the Love, Care, Share Foundation, which has a 'vision to make a positive difference in children's lives who are affected by poverty and suffering. The more we love, the more we care, the more we share, and together through positivity power we change the world.' She believes that her work with her foundation enables her on a daily basis to fulfil her life's purpose to do something for the greater good of mankind.

Here we will look at the following types of physical change:

- Remarkable healing
- Changes in electromagnetic field

Remarkable healing

Many accounts of NDEs from across the world include reports of seemingly 'miraculous' healing following an NDE. One such case is that of Mellen-Thomas Benedict, who in 1982 had been in hospice care for some months for the last stages of terminal cancer. He woke one morning at 4:30 am and knew he was going to die. He called his friends to say goodbye and called his hospice worker to instruct her not to move his body until six hours after he had died.

For an hour-and-a-half he appeared to have no vital signs. During this time he encountered a long and detailed NDE, in which he gained many insights into the nature of the universe and the interconnectivity of all things, past and future. When he finally came out of his NDE, Benedict found himself back in his body with his hospice worker looking over him crying – she'd had every reason to believe he was dead. Within three days Benedict had made a remarkable recovery. He felt completely normal. Three months later tests showed that his cancer had gone. What his doctors refer to as spontaneous remission, Benedict calls a miracle.

One of my own patients, whose hand was permanently contracted by the cerebral palsy he'd had from birth, could fully open out his hand for the first time following his NDE. Without surgery followed by extensive physiotherapy (neither of which my patient had had), doctors and physiotherapists could not explain how such a recovery could be possible.

Changes in electromagnetic field

Some physical after-effects may not even be discernible to the NDEr him- or herself. One such effect is a change in the person's electromagnetic field (see case study, page 90). I find this sort of change particularly fascinating because it is quantifiable – that is, we can measure it in some way. For example, some NDE accounts relay how after an experience the NDEr's watch may not work. There doesn't seem to be any logical reason why the watch would stop working. No particular type or price-bracket of watch seems immune from the effects – some really expensive, good-quality watches have been reported as malfunctioning on the NDEr but working perfectly well on the wrist of someone else.

Many NDErs have also described how lights will flicker on and off in their presence, kettles and toasters will blow up, and computers will frequently crash. And some NDErs have given accounts of store credit-card machines malfunctioning as they try to pay. It seems that their electromagnetic field has been disrupted to such an extent during the NDE that it also affects the electromagnetic field of electrical items that they come into contact with.

What other types of change are commonly reported?

We are generally able to categorize the main types of post-NDE change, but there are a few examples that fall outside our sphere of reference – perhaps they might be considered spiritual, but perhaps they go beyond even that:

• Being able to heal others
• Developing psychic tendencies

CASESTUDY ELECTRONIC MALFUNCTIONING

I was given the following report of the effects on one NDEr: 'Interestingly, I now can't wear watches as they just stop on me and I just don't like how they feel on my wrist. It's like the energy of them irritates me ... I also have always had problems with causing lights to flicker or explode, and electrical goods to stop working, but they work perfectly well for others.'

Being able to heal others

Some NDErs feel their experience has given them the ability to heal others. One lady wrote to me to tell me that, shortly after her NDE, she discovered that placing her hands over another person's injury promoted healing. She'd discovered her ability when she'd instinctively put her hands over the injured leg of her friend's cocker spaniel and, after a few minutes, the dog got up and was able to walk without even a limp. NDErs who have developed this ability report that healing is more a 'channelling' of energy than any new superhuman power.

Developing psychic tendencies

Accounts of NDEs tell us that some NDErs come away from the experience with new psychic abilities, especially the skill of premonition – becoming aware of events before they happen (see case study, page 93). Being able to 'see the future' in this way is commonly reported as one of the least welcome side-effects of an NDE, as people find the sense of knowing and responsibility that comes with it a burden.

Sometimes the improved empathy that can result from an NDE (see page 82) goes a step further: in some NDErs it becomes an ability to read the thoughts or energy of others (see case study, page 92).

The same subject who reported flickering lights and malfunctioning watches (see case study, page 90) also gave me the following after-effects of her NDE: 'I'm also very sensitive to some people's moods and can predict what has gone on in their lives and what will happen ... I don't see auras but I do feel in my body certain things like a heavy, thick fog around somebody who is depressed or not in a happy place ... and a feeling of expansion in my chest when somebody is really loving and kind. I get an idea of dizziness (but not an actual feeling, as such) when somebody is on drugs. I can 'feel' certain people even if they are not in the room, especially if I love them very much. I have a lot of predictive, vivid dreams or dreams that just give me information that I need to know about. It could just be my subconscious making sense of the world, but I have dreamt about things that have then come true.'

Could it be a sense of cheating death, rather than NDE, that leads to personal transformation?

Surviving a close brush with death or a life-threatening illness brings with it a natural reaction to re-evaluate your life and lifestyle. Who wouldn't, following a near-fatal accident or illness, want to thereafter live every moment as if it were their last? I know many people, including close friends, who've done just that. However, one controlled study compared the changes in those who'd had an NDE with those who'd had a brush with death without an NDE. The results seemed to show clearly that the subsequent physical, psychological and spiritual changes in the NDErs were more profound than in those who'd 'merely' been in mortal danger. The authors concluded that it was therefore the NDE itself and not the life-threatening situation that was the catalyst for significant change, which makes us want to ask again, what then really are NDEs and how can science explain them?

CASESTUDY **SEEING THE FUTURE**

I received one email from an NDEr who believes she had a premonition about the attacks on the Twin Towers in New York City, on 9 September, 2001. This was how she described it to me: 'It was not a visual flash – more like a feeling that tuned in my mind to it ... it's hard to describe. I felt a lot of people suffering ... screaming, "we're all gonna die"... I didn't know what that was until 9/11 happened. The tragedy affirmed to me that feeling I'd had.'

CHAPTER 5
Can science
explain NDEs?

Despite nearly four decades of research, no single scientific theory has yet been able to fully explain what causes NDEs. When we look at the full range of phenomena that comprise an NDE – from bright lights and feelings of tranquillity within the experience to apparently miraculous healing and the unshakeable need to change lives after it – can we really expect a tidy scientific explanation for NDEs? This chapter explores in more detail various theories about what could be considered to cause NDEs, taking a look at the limitations of scientific approaches first.

Could NDErs have been lacking oxygen or had other abnormal blood chemistry?

In this section we're going to examine the following possible physical causes of NDEs:

- Hypoxia
- Gravitational Loss of Consciousness (G-LOC)
- Hypercarbia

Hypoxia

A doctor once told me about an NDE he'd had as a child. During a tooth extraction at the dentist, he felt that he left his body and looked down at himself in the dentist's chair. Everything went black, except a light in the distance. Before he could move toward the light, he suddenly found himself back in the chair with a mouthful of blood and the dentist trying to wake him up. As he recounted the tale, he tried to rationalize it – he had been given gas to anaesthetize him during the extraction and he said this, in his opinion, had made him hypoxic (lacking in oxygen). The lack of oxygen, he believed, had led to the OBE and NDE.

As hypoxia gradually reduces brain function, increasing a sense of confusion, disorientation and disorganization rather than creating a lucid, heightened state of awareness like the one described, I don't think hypoxia alone is a sufficient explanation for an NDE. Plus, most people who come close to death are hypoxic – but they don't all report having NDEs.

Gravitational Loss of Consciousness (G-LOC)

As part of their training, pilots are exposed to accelerated speeds to prepare them for a common phenomenon called Gravitational Loss of Consciousness (G-LOC): at high speeds the heart loses its ability to pump blood efficiently around the body, which can lead to unconsciousness. During the exercise, pilots report experiences that resemble NDEs – a calm sense of well-being, OBEs, visions and a feeling of euphoria. However, these experiences appear to be random, often difficult to recall and are not life-changing. In these ways they are therefore distinct from NDEs.

Hypercarbia

A high level of carbon dioxide has also been mooted as an NDE trigger. Hypercarbic patients have reported seeing bright lights and geometric shapes, as well as having OBEs, and both lovely and distressing emotions. However, as with the hypoxic patients, hypercarbic patients exhibit and report none of the transformative effects of NDE.

My own findings

Finally, during my own research, I have seen and analyzed blood samples taken from NDErs. It was difficult to extract blood at the precise time that the NDE was occurring but in the few cases where this happened the oxygen levels were within normal limits. I have not seen any convincing evidence in any sample that indicates to me that blood chemistry in itself can cause NDEs.

Could certain medications trigger NDE?

During my hospital research I investigated whether NDEs were more common among patients taking either painkillers or sedatives. When I asked patients who'd been given these medications during their time in ITU, only 1 per cent reported having NDEs. Patients who'd never had either type of drug also reported them. And, of course many NDEs occurred outside a hospital setting, where no drugs had been administered at all. Overall, though, I found a result I wasn't expecting: drugs can actually impede or distort NDEs, turning them into something more confused. My own research has been corroborated by the work of other researchers.

Aren't OBEs associated with epilepsy? What about experiments that stimulate the brain to induce OBE?

OBEs have often been reported by people who experience epileptic seizures and those diagnosed with temporal lobe epilepsy. However, the OBEs in these people tend to differ slightly in their nature from those experienced by NDErs. Whereas a person with epilepsy may feel connected to and part of their body throughout the OBE, NDErs report that during their OBE they feel detached, existing outside their bodies. In addition, even though people with epilepsy feel part of their physical selves, they feel separate from the experience, as if watching a movie. NDErs, on the other hand, feel bound to the sensations of what's happening and in a heightened state of awareness.

Swiss doctor Olaf Blanke and his colleagues conducted a series of experiments to stimulate electromagnetically part of the brain (the gyrus) and induce OBEs. Although the research triggered a wave of articles claiming that at last we had a scientific explanation for OBEs, in fact the descriptions of the experiences given by the research subjects were quite different (more dreamlike, disconnected, vague and piecemeal) from the very specific, clear and detailed descriptions given of OBE during NDEs. Other research attempts, involving such things as electromagnetic fields to stimulate parts of the brain, have yet to prove robust enough to be convincing. Following one experiment researchers even concluded that the power of suggestion was more likely to produce OBE-like experiences than any electromagnetic stimulation.

Could NDEs simply be hallucinations?

Let's first define what we mean by hallucinations. This is what the Oxford English Dictionary tells us:

Hallucination

1. The mental condition of being deceived or mistaken, or of entertaining unfounded notions; an idea or belief to which nothing real corresponds; an illusion.
2. *Pathol. and Psychol.* The apparent perception (usually by sight or hearing) of an external object when no such object is actually present. (Distinguished from illusion in the strict sense, as not necessarily involving a false belief.)

During my nursing career I frequently saw hospital patients hallucinate. Often they would try to get out of bed, demonstrate feelings of paranoia and not let any medical staff near them. They'd sometimes try to remove intravenous lines and could even be aggressive toward members of staff. When they had recovered from the hallucination, they seldom had any memory of their behaviour. If they did, they were deeply embarrassed by their actions and described random, disjointed events pieced together from the reality of their situation. What the patients described was often the result of background noise and actual things that were happening at the time in the room – leading to a sort of warped reality manifesting in hallucination.

For example, I once witnessed a severely injured young man become convinced that people were trying to cut up his body and put it into boxes. At the same time he thought a man from the IRA was threatening him. Actually what happened (I was there and saw it) was that nurses restrained him as his painkiller sedatives wore off. In his confusion he became more aggressive. The so-called IRA member was really an Irish doctor who was trying to reassure him. This man was hallucinating – taking real events and making them unreal.

Contrary to the confused and disoriented states following a period of unconsciousness or when patients have been hallucinating, NDErs describe NDE as being a heightened state of awareness that is superior to their ordinary waking consciousness.

Knowledge acquired through NDEs

Other NDErs have described listening to conversations between people from whom they were separated by great distances. For example, during the initial stages of Dr Rajiv Parti's NDE (see page 49), he had found himself observing his mother talking to his sister at her home in India; at the time he was himself in California.

NDErs may also gain knowledge or skills during their experience. For example, one woman in my study came back to life only to have a acquired a detailed (and utterly remarkable) understanding of quantum physics!

Deathbed vision (DBV)

Another phenomenon that can occur close to death (and which may be questioned as a hallucination) is that of the dying person communicating with deceased relatives or friends. This experience is known as a deathbed vision (DBV).

Like NDEs, and in contrast to hallucinations, DBVs, which may occur anything from a week to a few days before a person dies, seem to be calm, serene and clearly articulated. Patients may gesticulate or 'talk' to someone in the room that no one else can see. Studies show that often these invisible people are significant figures from the patient's life, such as friends or family, who have already died.

One of the clearest examples of a DBV that I have seen occurred when I was working in ITU. I saw a patient begin to gesture, smile and talk to someone I couldn't see. He seemed so happy. He talked this way for about 30 minutes and then fell asleep. The following day he told his family that during the night he had been visited by his mother and grandmother, both of whom were dead, and also his sister. He couldn't understand why his sister would have been in his vision, though, seeing as far as he knew she was still alive. Of course, that wasn't the case – she'd died the week before, but his family had kept her death from him, for fear of upsetting him. A few days later he died entirely at peace.

Could endorphins explain NDEs?

Endorphins are among the body's natural painkillers – we commonly call them 'feel-good hormones'. It is not unreasonable to think that they could be responsible for NDEs because, for example, many athletes, during vigorous training or when they are competing, report having 'peak experiences' – or 'runner's high'. We know this to be the result of the release of endorphins during exercise. However,

FOCUS ON RESPONDING TO A DBV OR NDE

Before I became interested in NDEs, my grandfather was dying at home. I witnessed him on several occasions pointing to the doorway and telling me to look who was there. Of course, every time I looked at the doorway it was empty. My nurse training had taught me to reorient patients who were convinced that something unreal was real, so I always told my grandfather that there was no one there. Unsurprisingly, he used to become quite agitated at my refusal to believe him because as far as he was concerned, the presence in the doorway was completely real.

I now realize, with years of research under my belt, that the most important thing that we can do as onlookers of these experiences is to validate them, whatever our personal beliefs are. We should say things like 'Well I can't see anyone, but who can you see?' or 'What are they saying to you?' as this can help the person to have an easeful transition into death.

patients who have said that during their NDE they were pain-free (when in life they were experiencing pain) also say that when they re-enter their body the pain comes back immediately. Nothing in our physiology allows for the sudden disappearance of pain. Even if the body releases endorphins quickly, the pain-relief itself is gradual as the endorphins build up gradually in the circulation. Similarly, the effects of endorphins wear off gradually rather than immediately and spontaneously. For this reason, the sudden onset of pain following an NDE highlights that endorphins cannot be the sole cause of an NDE.

Could NDEs be some sort of vivid dream?

Studies show that we remember our dreams only if we wake during the period of our sleep when the dream is taking place; waking even during the next sleep phase makes a dream very hard to recall, certainly in any detail. And even if we do immediately remember a dream, the memory of it often fades very quickly. NDEs, on the other hand, are highly memorable and often life-changing, etched so deeply on the NDErs psyche that even the smallest details can seem vivid. Their impact on real life is dramatic and long-lasting.

However, while regular dreams do not have the necessary characteristics to identify them as a potential 'sidekick' of the NDE, my research is beginning to show that there are, in fact, interesting similarities between NDEs and lucid dreams. In a lucid dream the dreamer becomes aware that he or she is dreaming and can control the dream, making decisions within the scenario, averting or entering into, certain dream situations, or entering into them, changing outcomes, and bringing him- or herself out of the dream at will. This awareness and the ability to make decisions (to move toward the light, or back to life, for example) certainly have resonance with NDE. It might be that, in time, doing more research with lucid dreams will unlock some more concrete answers about the nature of NDE.

Are NDEs just wishful thinking – the result of our deep desire to reconnect with deceased loved ones?

Although the need to reconnect with lost loved ones might feasibly be considered a trigger for positive NDEs, we know that not all NDEs are positive or pleasant (see Chapter 2). Some may even be terrifying. No one can ever be certain that their NDE, if they have one, will be positive. And, none of my research subjects would have wanted to take the risk that their potentially final moments might be distressing or frightening. Furthermore, not every NDEr meets deceased loved ones, and several cases in my own research have revealed NDErs did not meet the relatives in their NDE who they would, when asked during life, most wish to meet. If wishful thinking were the trigger for an NDE, we would expect that the fulfilment of the wish – meeting our closest relatives rather than distant ones; and finding our fondest friends, rather than acquaintances – would be the likely outcome.

Where does all that leave us?

When it comes to trying to explain what really causes NDEs, the brutal truth is that although we are now much more open to the experience of NDEs and all that this entails, we are still not that much wiser than we were hundreds of years ago as to any hard, scientific answers. Science doesn't appear to offer us any realistic or robust answers – all we can do is keep researching, keep recording the experiences and talking about them, then analyze them as closely as we can to watch the patterns emerge.

However, just because our current science cannot explain NDEs does not mean that these are not real. I believe our inability to explain NDEs from this perspective is due to limitations in our scientific understanding as it currently stands, and that we need to review and expand our science rather than ignore these extremely important experiences. Recent research into NDEs just scratches the surface of what is to be learned about consciousness. Research in this area is increasing and the possibility of achieving a greater understanding is what excites me and inspires me to continue with my work.

CHAPTER 6

What can NDEs teach
those who've never
had one?

Twenty years ago, when I began my research into NDEs, I thought I would find all the answers. Today, when I think about what my research has taught me, I realize that for everything I've learned, there are still a lot more questions that need answering. Nonetheless, I have realized one important thing that is unrelated to what causes NDEs or what each one means: simply that each and every one of the stories from NDErs hold valuable lessons for all of us about the nature of living and dying, whether we've experienced an NDE ourselves or not.

Kenneth Ring, Professor of Psychology at the University of Connecticut, USA, called NDEs a 'benign virus'. As he taught students about the nature of these experiences and described the stories of transformation that had come from NDErs themselves, he witnessed a level of transformation among his students, too. None of these students had had their own NDE, they were merely 'feeding off' the positive effects of the stories they heard. I know from personal experience that engaging with and understanding NDEs can in itself lead to positive changes in the lives of those who want to learn about them. About 12 years ago, French journalist Sonia Barkallah found the same thing. In trying to overcome depression, Sonia came across an account of an NDE that intrigued her. As she delved more deeply into the subject, reading more and more NDE accounts, she found her depression lifting. The positive messages of the NDEs she was reading about began to turn her own life around. Now, all over the world she promotes the life-changing positive effects of the messages of NDE. Against the odds she has raised awareness of NDEs throughout France (organizing two big conferences) and has set up her own Internet site – itself providing a wonderful, ongoing resource for anyone fascinated by the subject of NDE.

How can NDEs transform our world view?

There are so many positive ways in which an NDE or learning about the NDEs of others can change our lives. During the course of my research I have observed that NDEs can encourage us to:

- Confront mortality and release fear
- Live life in the moment
- See the ripple effects of our actions on others
- Develop compassion

Confront mortality and release fear

There's no denying that NDEs force us to acknowledge our mortality. Accepting the existence of NDEs means accepting the inevitability of our own death. This is a key step to releasing our fear of death – we know death will happen, we accept it will happen and we know from the NDE accounts that it need not be anything to be afraid of. (Many NDErs believe that they have actually experienced death – they have already died, and now that they have come back to life they know what to expect when death does eventually come.) And it is a well-known psychological fact that when we confront our fears they usually begin to disappear.

Live life in the moment
It may sound like a cliché, but understanding that death really will come to us all has the knock-on effect of helping us to appreciate every moment, to live what can be called mindful lives. Learning about NDEs has taught me, for example, to make the most of my time with my parents, who live overseas. Not only am I aware of my own mortality, I'm aware of theirs, too. The effect also ripples beyond my closest relatives to experiences and friends: 'What if this is the last time I go to the beach?' and 'Would I be afraid to tell my friends how much they mean to me if this were the last day of my life?' NDEs can help us to learn to appreciate every moment as if it were our last.

NDEs often also remind us that we can't take our money and possessions with us when we die. Rather than being a slave to a job they don't enjoy or spend too long doing, or to the trappings of having money (see page 83), many NDErs learn to let go of possessions and instead value moments and experiences in the spirit of connected, mindful living.

FOCUS ON MAXIMIZING YOUR MOMENTS

Try this little exercise. Ask yourself: What if today were the last day of my life? And spend five minutes considering your answer. Use the following questions as prompts, but allow your thoughts to take you in their own direction, if you wish.

• Would you be doing something different to what you're doing right now? • Would you have planned your day differently? • What would you like to say to family and friends? • What experiences would you want to fit in – perhaps those you've been too embarrassed or intimidated to try; or those you've felt would make you feel or look silly? • What would you most like to eat?

Now think about what would flash before you if you were to have a life review (see page 28). What would be the stand-out moments from your life? What moments would be missing from the review – experiences you wish you'd made time for, but haven't yet? When you've finished considering how you can maximize your moments, go out and start creating those that are missing. Right now.

I read somewhere quite recently about a woman who'd gone for a walk in the park and got caught in a heavy rain shower. Everyone else in the park ran for cover, but she just stood there with open arms and a big smile, allowing the rain to fall over her head and body. When the shower had passed, someone asked her why she'd looked so happy. She replied that she had a terminal illness and was close to the end of her life and that may have been the last chance she had to experience rain.

See the ripple effects of our actions on others

NDErs who've had a life review often report powerful feelings of regret or nostalgia about how their own actions have been interpreted by or have affected others in their lives. This, surely, has to be one of the most significant lessons we can learn from NDErs – nothing we do is ever truly in isolation; our words and actions impact on those around us. If we can work toward that impact being positive, rather than negative, we can genuinely do our bit to change the world.

One easy way to weave this lesson into our everyday lives is to try a mini life review at the end of each day. Before you go to bed, think back over your day's thoughts, comments and actions and put yourself in the shoes of anyone who might have sensed, heard or witnessed them. For example, in the heat of the moment you might have responded angrily

CASESTUDY LEADING A FULFILLING LIFE

In 1993 Tibor Putnoki, a Hungarian pilot, had a cardiac arrest. His heartbeat was absent for nine minutes and during that time he had an extensive NDE. During the experience he faced three questions:

1. Did you have a life before your death?
2. Did you live a life worthy of a human being?
3. Could you look into other people's eyes with a pure heart and your head held high?

Tibor realized that, in order to live a fulfilling life, these were questions we should all ask ourselves every day. To that end he established The Light of Love Foundation, a non-profit organization that helps people to rebalance their lives physically, mentally, emotionally and spiritually. The foundation also promotes creative activities to enable people to value themselves, and offers courses on self-knowledge. Through working on practical projects, such as camping trips that encourage participants to help each other, he emphasizes community-building, teaching the value of working together as a human community, as well as working on self-improvement.

to someone, perhaps you even said something unkind. On reflection, when the heat has died down and you're conducting a mini life review, you might realize there was an alternative, more reasonable and considerate path to resolution. Reflecting on your thoughts, comments and actions each day using the life-review technique for self-awareness, then taking steps to modify your behaviour, can help to rewire your neural pathways so that responding calmly (rather than reacting in extreme ways, for example) becomes the default position, sending out positive ripples, rather than negative ones.

Develop compassion

Many NDErs, as part of their post-NDE transformation, find a deeper sense of compassion, of wanting to do good for others. Imagine how much more compassion and kindness there would be in the world if all of us could learn from this transformation! Try to develop your tolerance for others' ways of doing things. Try to respect others' choices. If someone reacts angrily or aggressively toward you, try to respond with kindness and respect, rather than your own anger or aggression. The impact on your life will be to create greater respect and understanding in your relationships with others; and greater overall happiness and peace.

FOCUS ON SHARING EMOTIONS

Kelly Walsh, founder of the Love, Care, Share Foundation (see pages 86–7), broke down during a radio interview in 2015 as she described her spiritually transformative experience (STE). In order to reassure all the supporters who were listening to her, afterwards she posted a short video to explain what had happened and why she had become so emotional. Her honesty, integrity and bravery triggered an influx of compassion from those who followed her on social media and were members of her forums. In effect, her having broken down live on air – and her subsequent sharing of emotions involved in this – taught even those who had not been through a STE or an NDE the importance of accepting and facing our emotions. In doing so she laid herself open to the comments of her community, and in response found compassion, love and respect. Kelly's example highlights the importance of NDErs being able to share their experiences with others in a supportive environment, and also for those who are listening to be compassionate as well as sympathetic to what the NDErs are trying to communicate.

CHAPTER 7

What are the wider
implications of knowing
more about NDEs?

In previous chapters we have looked at how learning about NDEs can impact on us as individuals – even individuals who haven't ourselves had any deep spiritual experiences. In this chapter we'll explore how a greater understanding of what NDEs are and how they impact on NDErs themselves, and on the other people around them, can improve the way we operate in the wider world – in offering the best possible healthcare and in looking after the environment, for example. We'll also go beyond these situations to ask questions of universal importance: Are NDEs evidence of life after death? And what can NDEs teach us about consciousness?

How can understanding NDEs improve healthcare?

NDEs are such personal experiences that it can be easy to overlook the fact that they also offer wider lessons about the formal care we give to others, both in hospital and at home. For example, NDEs show that we can help patients by doing the following:

- Allowing people to die with dignity
- Supporting NDErs as they process their experience
- Meeting the spiritual needs of patients

Allowing people to die with dignity

Being in hospital, not just for patients, but for family and friends, too, can be an unnerving, even scary experience.

When a loved one is in a life-threatening situation, being faced with the reality of the end of their life requires compassion, understanding and emotional and spiritual support from the people caring for both the patient and the families. Sadly, modern hospitals can be so busy, frantic and overstretched that these holistic aspects of healthcare provision are sometimes overlooked.

NDEs teach us of the importance of compassion in care for others. They teach us to respect the wishes of others in their final days and weeks, and they teach us to listen to and understand their wishes and the wishes of the family (see box, pages 130–31).

I have a personal hope that we will be able to extend these important humanitarian aspects of healthcare provision into the training we give our medical staff. I would like to see healthcare for terminally or fatally ill patients focused on the whole experience (not just the physical experience) of what it means to be faced with the prospect of death – of the self or a loved one. In this way we can help patients die with dignity, and improve the families' experience of mourning.

Supporting NDErs as they process their experience

As we've heard, processing the experience of an NDE is not always an easy task. Even if a person's NDE has been positive, the NDEr may feel isolated after the experience or otherwise misunderstood. Those who've had distressing NDEs can at times suffer a level of psychological disturbance, and it's essential we recognize the need to treat this with long-term psychological counselling. We also need to ensure that we draw the experiences from those who might be reticent to

FOCUS ON LETTING LIFE GO

My NDE research has transformed the way I think of death. Even in my own experience, I know that I had a completely different attitude to my grandmother's death – which came after my research – to that of my grandfather 16 years earlier. Before my research I believed wholeheartedly in the paramount importance of medical intervention to prolong life. My thoughts were that modern medicine could prevent my grandfather's death and that he should have surgical intervention even if he didn't want it. All my faith was in the medical system – I didn't look at the importance of having faith in the bigger picture. By the time it came to nursing my grandmother, I had learned that sometimes what the patient chooses is best. Death needs to be tranquil, dignified, calm. My grandmother didn't want surgery (and its associated significant risks) for her brain tumour, and

talk about them. Raising awareness of NDEs, learning about the nature of them in all their guises and then using that improved understanding in our healthcare provision for NDErs can speed up the process of integrating the experience positively into their lives. The more we know about NDEs and the more willing NDErs are to talk to us, the more able we are,

chose to die her own way. It wasn't what I wanted for her – I wanted her to go on living – but her death was inevitable and it was her wish. I didn't try to persuade her otherwise. Her death was a peaceful one.

Of course, sometimes it's the families, as well as the patients and their experiences, who have something to teach the medical staff about permitting dignity and respect in death. One 90-year-old woman was admitted to a hospital ward while I was on duty during my first-year training. She didn't want to be in hospital – her family had cared for her at home for two years, and she was now ready to die. She and all her family rejected the hospital's calls for intervention to prolong her life. Eventually, she was allowed to go home, where she died peacefully two days later. Who knows whether or not she had an NDE, but her sense of tranquillity can only have made death itself as serene as it could be.

or will be, to put like-minded individuals together to support each other, helping to remove any feelings of isolation.

Meeting the spiritual needs of our patients
NDEs appear to be proof that we are so much more than our physical bodies. In this way they teach us that in order to provide holistic healthcare, we need to meet our patients' spiritual needs, as well as their physical ones. Meeting spiritual needs does not necessarily mean providing religious guidance – spirituality is about connecting with our patients on an emotional and soulful level. Being given the opportunity to listen to music, having family at the bedside all day, reading a religious text or a book of poetry, may be all that's needed to access and enrich a person's spirituality in the broadest sense. Good healthcare provision should be about opening our ears to our patients' spiritual needs and doing everything we can to meet them. This isn't just for those who are dying, but for all those who need medical care (see box, pages 130–31).

The examples of those NDErs who shared their experiences with other critically ill patients in hospital (see pages 81–2) really underlines how considering the spiritual side of a person's wellbeing can empower those who are sick to take an active role in their recovery, hastening it toward the most positive outcome possible.

How can improved understanding of NDEs impact our environment, our planet?

NDEs can highlight the interconnectivity of all things (see pages 85–6) – of people, of animals, of objects, of the environment. Many NDErs report how their experience gave them insight into the effects of human action not only on other people, but also on the world around them. This new way of understanding our interdependence is often the result of a life review (see pages 26–7). An NDEr's focus may widen from their own self, to see themselves as just one part of the interconnected whole that is our planet.

This perspective is aligned with the viewpoint of many indigenous cultures, whose people have a deep respect for the land and animals that support them, and whose traditional ways of life entail taking only what they need and giving thanks for what they receive. In contrast to traditional ways of nurturing resources, modern society seems out of control, acting for immediate gain without thinking of the impact on other people, future generations and the world itself. NDErs who have experienced directly the interconnectivity of life can educate us about the importance of issues such as controlling climate change and protecting our food chain. Their experiences invite us to look at the wider perspective and examine how our lives impact our planet.

Are NDEs evidence of life after death?

When I began researching NDEs, proof of any life after death was not something I had in mind. I conducted my research so that I could have a better understanding of the dying process (rather than of what happens once death has occurred), and so that I could do my bit to improve the provision for dying patients in hospitals, hospices and at home.

However, this topic without doubt has potentially far-reaching implications for NDErs, and has prompted many people to contact me. On the one hand, the fact that some NDErs relay that they have met, talked to or simply seen deceased relatives during their experiences suggests that life after death must exist (and remember that sometimes the NDEr doesn't even know that the person they've seen during the experience is actually dead, and sometimes they describe deceased family members they've never met or even seen in photographs).

On the other hand, if we are talking about life after death as a continuation of life as we know it, carried on in another realm, the NDE research still leaves many unanswered questions. We may never know for certain whether NDEs are evidence of life after death, but until we do I believe that we have to keep a open mind and keep on asking questions.

What can NDEs teach us about consciousness?

When we consider the question of whether or not NDEs are some sort of confirmation of life after death, I think it is more important to ask the question 'What is consciousness?' My personal belief is that the body and the brain are not the producers of all things – they aren't the initiators, they don't come first – but that life begins with consciousness. This seems to be indicated by research into NDEs. If consciousness is produced by the brain then there should be no experience when someone has a cardiac arrest. Yet hospital research undertaken and published since 2001 shows that people whose brains are not receiving oxygen are reporting clear, lucid and heightened states of awareness.

One way of explaining NDEs is to explore the possibility that consciousness is primary and 'non-local' (not localized in the brain). The heightened state of consciousness experienced by NDErs is constantly around us and within us, but we are not aware of it because the brain filters it out. However, there are times in our life when our brains become physiologically impaired – for example, when we are approaching death or during a near-death event. The brain's filter action subsequently relaxes and rather than creating an experience, it merely allows this heightened state of consciousness to be experienced in its entirety.

This way of thinking about consciousness makes sense to me and has yet wider implications for the way we live. It opens the possibility for a profound understanding of the interconnectedness of all people and things, as sensed by so many NDErs during life reviews. It is remarkable how many NDErs are inspired by their experience to examine the repercussions of their actions on other people and on the

FOCUS ON **CREATING A DEATH PLAN**

Most people tend not to give death much real thought until we are confronted with it. NDEs highlight the preciousness of life; they show us that we seldom consider or pay attention to things that will have great relevance to us at the point of our death. When we read about others' experiences of NDEs, we're reminded that the process of dying is in itself a part of our life and something that, like anything else, would benefit from a plan.

A death plan enables any matter, large or small, relating to the way in which we want to die (who we want around us, what treatment we do or don't want and so on) to become a conscious decision taken during life. This helps to release some of the fear around death – all is in order, all is calm.

world around them. If we could only live from the perspective of being deeply interconnected with others, then we would live in permanent consideration of love, compassion and co-operation – and that would be a truly beneficial way forward for humankind.

For this reason death plans (also called advanced care plans) are increasingly becoming an important part of nursing care. Good communication with family, the doctors, the district nurse and other relevant members of the medical team can ensure a more positive experience for a person who is dying.

It is important to remember that a death plan is not legally binding – it is only a list of wishes and preferences. Nonetheless, a death plan, carefully written and respectfully acknowledged by those who will be caring for you, can help to ease the transition from life to death, both for the person dying and for loved ones. Most doctors will be happy to keep your death plan with your medical notes if you choose. Just remember to update it if you change your mind about aspects of your care.

FOCUS ON IMPROVING SPIRITUAL INTELLIGENCE IN THE CARE OF THE TERMINALLY ILL

Every patient's spirituality is unique. Here are some guidelines to help you hone your own spiritual intelligence, whether you are a healthcare provider in a medical setting, or a family member caring for a dying relative.

RECOGNIZE the signs of spiritual unease: Often a dying patient's fidgetiness is interpreted as pain or physical discomfort. Naturally, we are inclined to reach for painkillers or sedatives to restore calm. However, my research shows that agitation is often the result of some kind of emotional distress – perhaps unfinished business, regret over past actions, or anxiety over who is being left behind. Talk through the emotional significance of what is happening, keeping medication to the minimum necessary. Allow the patient enough awareness for final words or resolutions.

VALIDATE visions: If a patient or loved one appears to see or talk to someone who is not visible to you, don't dismiss them. Validate them by asking for more details. Research shows that deathbed visions (DBVs) can be instrumental for a peaceful death, offering great comfort to those who are dying. To be told they aren't real can only cause agitation.

Sometimes, if the person isn't yet ready for death, DBVs are unwelcome or unwanted. Keep asking questions, searching for the content of what your loved one or patient is seeing. Offer reassurance if necessary. Often, as a patient becomes more accepting that death is coming, their attitude toward unwanted DBVs can improve.

EMPOWER through knowledge: Learning about NDEs can teach us about the experience of death, reducing fear and enabling families and healthcare providers to offer reassurance. Learning about the positive spiritual aspects of death can also be empowering, helping families to feel more able to nurse their loved ones through the last days of their lives at home, rather than in a hospital.

BECOME a 'soul midwife': Felicity Warner, founder of Soul Midwives in the UK, promotes holistic support for the terminally ill. You don't need medical training to become a soul midwife, just a willingness to facilitate a peaceful transition into death and to communicate the wishes of the dying person. The soul midwife may also help the dying person create a 'death plan' (see box, pages 128–9), which can cover anything from who the patient wishes to care for them at the end of their life, and whether family should be present, to whether he or she wants flowers in the room.

What next?

A person who can gather information during apparent lack of consciousness – information that cannot have been gathered or gleaned in any logical way – is a person who helps prove to us that consciousness is more than the product of grey matter and a beating heart. With this understanding comes the most important message of all – that we need to open our hearts, minds and spirit to the possibilities of interconnectivity, heightened states of awareness and spiritual empathy. Engaging with the messages of NDE accounts, seeking out NDErs and listening to what they have to say, and reflecting on their deep understanding of the nature of living and dying are all ways in which we can open ourselves to new spiritual awareness and personal fulfilment.

I hope that our greater understanding of NDEs will have a profound impact on our care for the terminally ill and dying. I would like doctors and nurses to have a greater understanding of what it means to be close to death, and to be able to recognize and appropriately respond to NDEs.

Already many school pupils are learning about NDEs as part of their curriculum. Introducing the topic at a young age helps broaden minds and challenge assumptions and forces us to dig deeper into our holistic understanding. Not only that, but the messages of NDEs can filter into a younger generation to engender the spirit of compassion and kindness at the most open-minded time of life.

One of the most valuable knock-on effects of our interest in NDEs will be that more NDErs will be willing to share their stories, feel validated, and process their experiences for the good of themselves and even of humanity.

We live in exciting times. Each step forward in our understanding of our innate interconnectivity produces a huge leap in protecting our evolutionary right to work and live together in harmony. We can become more selfless, more considerate, more mindful and more empathic. We will have more respect for our immediate environment and our planet as a whole. We will help to promote physical wellness, mutual respect and emotional and psychological well-being. We will nurture potential in our children. We will reduce disease and prolong happy, fulfilling lives – while promoting dignity and respect for those who are dying. We will no longer fear death.

I hope that you are as excited by these possibilities as I am and that you marvel, like I do, at just how life-affirming and inspiring NDEs can be.

Further reading

Atwater, P. M. H. (1992). 'Is There a Hell? Surprising observations about the near-death experience'. *Journal of Near-Death Studies*, Vol. 10, pp.149–160.

Atwater, P. M. H. (1999). *Children of the New Millennium: Children's Near-Death Experiences and the Evolution of Humankind*. New York: Three Rivers Press.

Ayer, A. J. (1988a). 'That Undiscovered Country/What I Saw When I Was Dead'. The *Sunday Telegraph*, 28 August 1988.

Ayer, A. J. (1988b). 'Postscript to a Postmortem'. *The Spectator*, 15 October 1988.

Bailey, L. W. and Yates, J. eds (1996). *The Near-Death Experience: A Reader*. New York, London: Routledge.

Benedict, Mellen-Thomas (1996). 'Through the Light and Beyond'. In Bailey and Yates, 1996, pp.39–52.

Berndt, R. and Berndt, C. (1989). *The Speaking Land: Myth and Story in Aboriginal Australia*. Harmondsworth: Penguin. (Cited in Kellehear, 1993, 2005.)

Blanke, O., Ortigue, S., Landis, T. and Seeck, M. (2002). 'Stimulating illusory own-body perceptions'. *Nature*, September, Vol. 419, p.269.

Blanke, O., Landis, T., Spinelli, L. and Seeck, M. (2004). 'Out-of-body experience and autoscopy of neurological origin'. *Brain*, Vol. 127, pp.243–258.

Bockie, S. (1993). *Death and the invisible powers: The world of Kongo belief*. Bloomington, IN: Indiana University Press.

Burpo, T. with Vincent, L. (2010). *Heaven is for Real*. Nashville, Dallas, Mexico City, Rio De Janeiro: Thomas Nelson.

Bush, N. E. (2002). 'Afterward: Making Meaning After a Frightening Near-Death Experience'. *Journal of Near-Death Studies*. Winter, Vol. 21 (2), pp.99–133.

Bush, N. E. (2012). *Dancing Past the Dark: Distressing Near-Death Experiences*. eBook Artisans.

Corazza, O. (2008). *Near-Death Experiences: Exploring the Mind-Body Connection*. Routledge, London and New York.

Counts, D. (1983). 'Near-Death and Out-of-Body Experiences in a Melanesian Society'. *Anabiosis*, Vol. 3, pp.115–135.

Delog Dawa Drolma (1995). *Delog: Journey to Realms Beyond Death*. Junction City, California: Padma Publishing.

Evans-Wentz, W. Y. (1960). *The Tibetan Book of the Dead*. London: Oxford University Press. First published in 1927.

Fenimore, A. (1995). *Beyond the Darkness: My Near Death Journey to the Edge of Hell and Back*. London, Sydney, New York, Tokyo, Singapore and Toronto: Simon and Schuster.

Fracasso, C. and Friedman, H. (2012). 'Electromagnetic Aftereffects of Near-Death Experiences: A Preliminary Report on a Series of Studies Currently Under Way'. *Journal of Transpersonal Research*, Vol. 4 (2), pp.34–55.

Gomez-Jeria, J. S. (2006). 'The Near-Death Experience in Pu Songling's Strange Stories from Liaozhai's Studio'. *Journal of Near-Death Studies*, Winter, Vol. 25 (2), pp.113–120.

Green, J.T. (1984). 'Near-death experiences in a Chamorro culture'. *Vital Signs*, Vol. 4 (1–2), pp.6–7.

Grey, M. (1987). *Return From Death: An Explanation of the Near-Death Experience*. London and New York: Arkana.

Greyson, B. and Bush, N. E. (1992). 'Distressing near-death experiences'. *Psychiatry: Interpersonal and Biological Processes*. Vol. 55 (1), pp.95–110.

Greyson, B. (2003). 'Incidence and correlates of near-death experiences in a cardiac care unit'. *General Hospital Psychiatry*, Vol. 25, pp.269–276.

Grof, S. (1994). *Books of the Dead: Manuals for Living and Dying*. Thames and Hudson.

Groth-Marnat, G. and Summers, R. (1998). 'Altered Beliefs, Attitudes, and Behaviour Following Near-Death Experiences.' *Journal of Human Psychology*, Vol. 38, pp.110–25.

Holden, J. M. (1988). 'Visual Perception During Naturalistic Near-Death Out-of-Body Experiences'. *Journal of Near-Death Studies*. Winter, Vol. 7 (2), pp.107–120.

Holden, J. M. (1989) 'Unexpected Findings in a Study of Visual Perception During the Naturalistic Near-Death Out-of-Body Experience'. *Journal of Near-Death Studies*. Spring, Vol. 7 (3), pp.55–163.

Holden, J. M. and Joesten, L. (1990). 'Near-Death Veridicality Research in the Hospital Setting: Problems and Promise'. *Journal of Near-Death Studies*. Fall, Vol. 9 (1), pp.45–54.

Kellehear, A. (1993). 'Culture, biology and the Near Death Experience'. *The Journal of Nervous and Mental Disease*. Vol. 181 (3), pp.148–156.

Kellehear, A. (2008). 'Census of Non-Western Near-Death Experiences to 2005: Overview of the Current Data'. *Journal of Near-Death Studies*, Summer, Vol. 26 (4), pp.249–265.

King, M. (1985). *Being Pakeha: An Encounter with New Zealand and the Maori Renaissance*. Auckland: Hodder and Stoughton.

La Tourelle, M. (2015). *The Gift of Alzheimer's: New Insights into the Potential of Alzheimer's and its Care*. London: Watkins Publishing.

Lawrence, M. (1995). 'The Unconscious Experience'. *American Journal of Critical Care*. Vol. 4 (3), pp.227–232.

Lawrence, M. (1998). *In a World of their Own: Experiencing Unconsciousness*. Westport, Connecticut, London: Bergin and Garvey.

Long, J and J. NDERF: www.nderf.org

McClenon, J. (2006). 'Kongo Near-Death Experiences: Cross-Cultural Patterns'. *Journal of Near-Death Studies*, Autumn, Vol. 25 (1), pp.21–34.

McCormack, I. www.aglimpseofeternity.org

Moody, R. A., Jnr. (1975). *Life After Life*. New York: Mockingbird/Bantam Books.

Morse, M. with Perry, P. (1993). *Transformed by the Light*. London: Piatkus.

Morse, M. (2000). *Where God Lives: The Science of the Paranormal and How Our Brains are Linked to the Universe*. New York: Cliff Street Books, an Imprint of Harper Collins Publishers.

Murphy, T. (2001). 'Near Death Experiences in Thailand'. *Journal of Near death Studies*. Vol. 19 (3), pp.161–178.

Nahm, M. and Nicolay, J. (2010). 'Essential Features of Eight Published Muslim Near-Death Experiences: An Addendum to Joel Ibrahim Kreps's "The Search for Muslim Near-Death Experiences"'. *Journal of Near-Death Studies*, Vol. 29 (1), pp.255–263.

Neihardt, J. G. (1995). *Black Elk Speaks*. Lincoln and London, University of Nebraska Press. Eighth cloth printing. Originally published New York: William Morrow & Company, 1932.

Nicholls, G. (2012). *Navigating the Out-of-Body Experience: Radical New Techniques*. Minnesota: Llewellyn Publications.

Parnia, S., Waller, D. G., Yeates, R., Fenwick, P. (2001). 'A qualitative and quantitative study of the incidence, features and aetiology of near death experiences in cardiac arrest survivors'. *Resuscitation*, Vol. 48, pp.149–156.

Parnia, S., Spearpoint, K., de Vos, G., Fenwick, P. et al (2014) 'AWARE – AWAreness during Resuscitation – A prospective study'. *Resuscitation* (in press accepted 7th September 2014).

Parti, R. www.drparti.com

Pasricha, S. and Stevenson, I. (1986). 'Near Death Experiences in India: A Preliminary Report'. *The Journal of Nervous and Mental Disease*. Vol. 174 (3), pp.165–170.

Pasricha, S. K. (2008). 'Near-Death Experiences in India: Prevalence and New Features'. *Journal of Near-Death Studies*, Summer, Vol. 26 (4), pp.267–282.

Persinger, M. (1987). *The Neuropsychological Bases of God Beliefs*. Praeger, New York.

Persinger, M. A. (2003b). 'Experimental Simulation of the God Experience: Implications for Religious Beliefs and the Future of the Human Species'. In R. A. Joseph (ed) *Neurotheology: Brain, Science, Spirituality, Religious Experience*. San José, California: University Press.

Putnoki, T. (2014). *9 Minutes: My Path to the Light/9 Perc: Utam a Fenybe*. Budapest: Szeretet Fenye Kozhaszu Alapitvany.

Rawlings, M. (1979). *Beyond Death's Door...* London: Sheldon Press. Third Impression. First published in the United States in 1978 by Thomas Nelson Inc., Publishers, Nashville, Tennessee.

Ring K. (1980). *Life at Death: A Scientific Investigation of the Near-Death Experience*. New York: Coward, McCann and Geoghegan.

Ring, K. (1992). *The Omega Project: Near-Death Experiences, UFO Encounters and Mind at Large*. New York, NY: William Morrow.

Ring, K and Valarino, E. (1998). *Lessons from the Light*. New York and London: Insight Books, Plenum Press.

Rommer, B. (2000). *Blessing in Disguise: Another Side of the Near-Death Experience*. Minnesota, USA: Llewellyn Publications.

Sabom, M. (1982). *Recollections of Death: An Investigation Revealing Striking New Medical Evidence of Life After Death*. London: Corgi. First Publication in Great Britain.

Sabom, M. (1998). *Light and Death: One Doctor's Fascinating Account of Near-Death Experiences*. Grand Rapids, Michigan: Zondervan Publishing House. A Division of Harper Collins Publishers.

Sartori, P., Badham, P. and Fenwick, P. (2006). 'A Prospectively Studied Near-Death Experience with Corroborated Out-of-Body Perceptions and Unexplained Healing'. *Journal of Near-Death Studies*, Winter, Vol. 25 (2), pp.69–84.

Sartori, P. (2008). *The Near-Death Experiences of Hospitalized Intensive Care Patients: A Five Year Clinical Study*. The Edwin Mellen Press, New York and Lampeter.

Sartori, P. (2014). *The Wisdom of Near-Death Experiences: How Understanding NDEs Can Help Us Live More Fully*. London: Watkins Publishing.

Schwaninger, J., Eisenberg, P. R., Schechtman, K. B. and Weiss, A. N. (2002). 'A Prospective Analysis of Near-Death Experiences in Cardiac Arrest Patients'. *Journal of Near-Death Studies.* Summer, Vol. 20 (4), pp.215–232.

Stone, Sharon interview with Oprahhttps://www.youtube.com/watch?v=xnHK6TbZTX0 *The Oprah Winfrey Show*, OWN TV. Original broadcast: 27 May 2004.

Storm, H. (2000). *My Descent into Death*. Clairview Books, London, UK.

Thrum, T. (1907). *Hawaiian Folk Tales: A Collection of Native Legends*. Chicago, IL: A. C. McClurg.

Thurman, R.A.F., (1994). *The Tibetan Book of the Dead: Liberation through understanding in the between*. London: Thorsons, an imprint of HarperCollins Publishers.

Van Lommel, P., van Wees, R., Meyers, V. and Eifferich, I. (2001). 'Near-death experience in survivors of cardiac arrest: a prospective study in the Netherlands'. *The Lancet,* 15 December, Vol. 358, pp.2039–2045.

Vecsey, C. and Venables, R. W. (eds) (1994). *American Indian Environments: Ecological Issues in Native American History*. New York: Syracuse University Press.

Wallis Budge, E. A. (1989). *The Book of the Dead*. London: Arkana. First published in Great Britain by Kegan Paul, Trench, Trubner 1899.

Warner, F. (2011). *A Safe Journey Home: A Simple Guide to Achieving a Peaceful Death*. London: Hay House.

Warner, F. (2013). *The Soul Midwives' Handbook: The Holistic and Spiritual Care of the Dying*. London: Hay House.

Warner, L. (1937). *A Black Civilization: A social study of an Australian tribe*. New York: Harper and Brothers (cited in Kellehear 2008).

Zaleski, C. (1988). *Otherworld Journeys: Accounts of near-death experience in medieval and modern times*. Oxford University Press.

Zhi-ying, F. and Jian-xun, Liu. (1992). 'Near-Death Experiences Among Survivors of the 1976 Tangshan Earthquake'. *Journal of Near-Death Studies*. Autumn, Vol. 11 (1), pp.39–49.

Further information

The definition for 'hallucination' in Chapter 5 comes from the OED online edition (accessed 23.04.15)

For more about Sonia Barakallah, founder of S17 Productions, please visit https://en.s17.tv

For more information about Kelly Walsh's Love, Care, Share Foundation, please visit www.positivityprincess.com

Acknowledgments

I would like to thank all of the people who have supported me since I began my research. There are too many to name individually but I will always be particularly grateful to my husband, Enrico, for putting up with my obsession with NDEs for the past 20 years and for being such a great dad to our son, Sol, while I've been busy with the writing of this book.

I'd also like to thank my family and friends for listening to my incessant chatter about NDEs, as well as Professor Paul Badham, Dr Peter Fenwick and the Alister Hardy Society for their continued support, and thank you to Graham Nicholls for sharing his knowledge about inducing OBEs in Chapter 1. A big thank-you to all at Watkins Media, especially Michael Mann for taking the time to read my first manuscript and believing in it, Etan Ifeld, Jo Lal, Deborah Hercun, Kelly Thompson, Vicky Hartley, Steph Bryant and the rest of the team. Thank you also to Judy Barratt for the editing of the manuscript.

Most importantly, I would like to thank all the people who have written to me and emailed me over the years to share their experiences with me (and for their permission to use their experiences in my publications) – they have been my greatest teachers.

ABOUT THE AUTHOR

DR PENNY SARTORI

One of the world's leading experts on NDEs, Dr Penny Sartori has a unique perspective on the phenomenon gained through her work as an intensive care nurse for almost 20 years. During that time she undertook the UK's first long-term prospective study of NDEs, interviewing patients in her care, and in 2005 was awarded a PhD for her research. She continues to research and lecture about NDEs all over the world and currently works at Swansea University.

ABOUT THE SERIES

We hope you've enjoyed reading this book.

If you'd like to find out more about other therapies, practices and phenomena that you've heard of and been curious about, then do take a look at the other titles in our thought-provoking **#What Is** series by visiting www.whatisseries.com

#WHATIS

The growing list of dynamic books in this series will allow you to explore a wide range of life-enhancing topics – sharing the history, wisdom and science of each subject, as well as its far-reaching practical applications and benefits.

With each guide written by a practising expert in the field, this new series challenges preconceptions, demystifies the subjects in hand and encourages you to find new ways to lead a more fulfilled, meaningful and contented life.

WATKINS

Sharing Wisdom Since
1893

The story of Watkins Publishing dates back to March 1893, when John M. Watkins, a scholar of esotericism, overheard his friend and teacher Madame Blavatsky lamenting the fact that there was nowhere in London to buy books on mysticism, occultism or metaphysics. At that moment Watkins was born, soon to become the home of many of the leading lights of spiritual literature, including Carl Jung, Rudolf Steiner, Alice Bailey and Chögyam Trungpa.

Today our passion for vigorous questioning is still resolute. With over 350 titles on our list, Watkins Publishing reflects the development of spiritual thinking and new science over the past 120 years. We remain at the cutting edge, committed to publishing books that change lives.

DISCOVER MORE ...

Read our blog

Watch and listen to
our authors in action

Sign up to
our mailing list

JOIN IN THE CONVERSATION

 WatkinsPublishing   @watkinswisdom

WatkinsPublishingLtd   +watkinspublishing1893

Our books celebrate conscious, passionate, wise and happy living.
Be part of the community by visiting

www.watkinspublishing.com